The Perfect School

Jim Rosborg

Max McGee

Jim Burgett

For additional information about this topic and the authors, please visit the website at
www.superintendents-and-principals.com

Printed book version:
ISBN 0-910167-90-7
ISBN 978-0-910167-90-1

Cover design by Douglas Burgett

Table of Contents

DEDICATIONS

Jim Rosborg

To my wife, Nancy, for being my best friend and supporter, and to our children, Carol, Kyle and his wife Barbi, Mike and his wife Wendy, and to our grandchild, Bradley, who together have brought so much happiness to my life and have made me give thanks for family every day.

Max McGee

To my greatest teachers: Dr. Phil Jackson of the University of Chicago, for his thought-provoking reading, lectures, and discussion and for the rigorous demands for intellectual discourse and the written word; my wife, Jan Fitzsimmons, whose work with the boys and girls of North Lawndale and East Aurora and future teachers for high needs schools has made an enormous tangible difference; my children, Joey, Mike, and Jess, and my grandson, Trent, whose patience, perspective, and playfulness humble and ground me in what matters most.

Jim Burgett

I dedicate this book to my family. To my parents who, without a doubt, loved the four of us and wanted us to make a difference in this world. To my wife, kids, their spouses, and my grandkids who make life worth living. I could not have found a better wife nor could we have more loving and caring kids...and they are growing their own crop very well. To my mother-in-law, Ruth, who I have kidded more times than I can count, but who is, and has always been, nothing short of wonderful. To my sister, Nancy, who was blessed with many, many talents and has a heart of gold. To brothers, Bill and Gordon, twins at birth, but who provide the full spectrum of values and ideals. Both are accomplished authors, both make this world a better place. And to Pat Schwarm, whom we consider family. Her influence on me as an educator and as a human cannot be measured.

ACKNOWLEDGMENTS

The authors wish to acknowledge the following people for their assistance in the research, development, and production of this book:

Jim Rosborg

Dr. Rick Acuncius, Dr. Joe Cipfl, Tim Cochran, Dr. Jeff Dosier, Evelyn Duncan, Heather Fouts, Marcy Gibson, Laurie Hubble, Brian James, Melissa Meeker, Tom Mentzer, Jennifer Moehrs, Debbie Murphy, Dennis O'Neill, Bill Porzukowiak, Jennifer Relleke, Carol Rosborg, Nancy Rosborg, Tracy Ross, LaDonna Singleton, Jennifer Stokes, Sabrina Storner, and Ryan Wamser. I would like to also acknowledge my McKendree College graduate classes whose discussions helped stimulate my thoughts for this book: Cahokia, Carterville, Fairview Heights, Granite City, Mascoutah, Mt. Vernon, and O'Fallon.

Max McGee

I am especially indebted to the teachers, staff, administrators, Board of Education, and parents of Wilmette District 39. All they have done to "teach tomorrow's leaders" served as the inspiration for this book. Toni Shinners, former principal of one of the perfect schools, showed perfection was possible, and all the principals of Illinois' Golden Spike Schools made the impossible achievable. God bless you.

Jim Burgett

The only thing I know about the vision of a perfect school I learned from others. The following list of folks served as personal mentors for different reasons: Bill Hyten, Kent Hammer, Dean Buckingham, Max McGee, Jim Rosborg, Mr. Ruggles, Pat Schwarm, Dennis Brueggemann, Brad Albrecht, Darell Bellm, Rick Acuncius, Terry Bauer, Wayne Krohmer, and Fred Singleton. These folks have, in some special way, taken the time over the years to share their passion for our profession with me personally. Each, in his or her own way, took a stand or made a difference. This group includes some teachers I had when I was a student, fellow administrators, and Board members. Most on this list became special friends. They taught me more than even they may ever realize. I also admire each of them for having the courage to take the risks necessary to move their schools forward on the road of excellence, headed toward perfection. They each made a difference in my life and I will always be grateful.

Introduction

Does a book with the title of "The Perfect School" need an introduction? If so, one that is mercifully short so you can get to the meat and purpose of its pages...

The first chapter asks "A Perfect School?" and begs the authors to reply. That there are 12 more chapters suggests that their replies are positive!

Is there or will there ever be a "perfect" school? Probably not, they say, but some are close, we have the tools and knowledge to move in that direction, the quest really is the journey, and a better word is "excellence," which is attainable and lies along that path to perfection.

Anyway, if perfection were attainable, would it be absolute or malleable, and if the latter, wouldn't we just keep reforming it to be even more perfect?

The chapters that follow are less philosophical or esoteric. They say that if we want to climb that path of excellence toward perfection, here's what we might think or do. Practical, tangible things. Whether discussing parents, teachers, staff, principals, service, character, perception, teaching, data, finances, or curriculum, the vision of what a perfect school would look like and what we can do to race or tiptoe up that glorious rise to see and live it are shared, for discussion and action.

And who dares even address perfection in education? Jim Rosborg, Max McGee, and Jim Burgett aren't long-bearded gods pronouncing from on high but rather roll-up-your-sleeves mortals with 100+ years of highly successful, much heralded labors in the fields of learning: all were teachers, principals, and superintendents, and much more. Their biographies near the back of the book will fill in the glorious gaps.

Too much introduction already. Let's let those daring souls pass their torches of excellence to you on the road to perfection, to ignite your own fires for today's learners—and for all learners forever.

Gordon Burgett, Publisher

Chapter One

A Perfect School?

Jim Rosborg, Max McGee, and Jim Burgett

How often have you attempted to create a perfect school? Fess up.

When did your Board last debate this very topic and either vote for its immediate and unwavering application to your entire district or asked you why it hadn't already been achieved?

Are your parents clamoring for perfect teachers, perfect classrooms, and a perfect curriculum?

Are your teachers making the very same demands—with the addition of perfect parents and perfect students?

Yet that's what we all want, isn't it? Isn't that your wish every time you make a decision?

Maybe the problem is the word "perfect."

Some things simply are perfect. Round is perfect. And a perfect redundancy is to describe something as "perfectly round"—it is or it isn't.

If something does precisely what it is designed to do every time, it is perfect. But if there are two or 22 variables and any one of them alters that precision, TILT. Imperfection!

And when can we control every variable (some days, any variable) in a school, district, classroom, teaching process, budget allocation, you name it? So speaking of perfection is about as realistic as turning desk-bottom gum into letters of praise or endless fun chits to be spent at will after retirement.

So why are three grizzled yet kindly and reputedly wise senior educators (with 100+ years of bottom-to-top, much heralded experience in K-12 education)[1] wasting their time and yours by proposing "the perfect school"?

And wouldn't it make perfect sense to skip this book for something that will yield at least sensible results?

Let's ask them, and you be the judge.

In fact, let's go a step further. Read this book, then let us know your ideas (with near-perfect succinctness, please) about "a perfect school." Please send your thoughts to www.superintendents-and-principals.com/mythoughts.htm.

Is a perfect school achievable?

Jim Rosborg: Everyone wants perfection in his field of expertise. That usually takes the form of changes (or improvements) that move a school in the direction of perfection. We've seen a multitude of changes in the attempt to improve the educational outcomes of students, yet most of those attempts at change (and the changes themselves) have had good intentions but limited results.

Change is certainly not new to education. As a matter of fact, when I first began teaching in 1972, a 91-year-old retired teacher named Glenn Brasel told me, "Jim, the first time change comes around to do the same thing you have already done in your career, simply deal with it and move on. The second time that change comes around, it's time to retire!" He was right. I had seen the same changes come and go, and return and go, when I retired in 2005.

Are things better now than then? Yes. Are they perfect? No. But we are closer.

Max McGee: A school that's perfect for parents will probably be imperfect for teachers. A school that's perfect for students will surely be far from perfect for the principal. The perfect school for the superintendent probably doesn't look like a perfect school for those taxpayers without children in it. Like great beauty, the per-

---

[1] The authors—Jim Rosborg, Max McGee, and Jim Burgett—wrote *What Every Superintendent and Principal Needs to Know*. Its revised and updated second edition was released in early 2007. See their full biographies before this book's Index.

fect school may be in the eye of the beholder. Neither is "achievable" but we'll know them—perfection and beauty—when we experience them.

Jim Burgett: A one-word answer is no, but achieving perfection is not the point of this book. This book is about a journey, not a destination. It is about how to become better, how to strive for perfection, not necessarily how to reach it.

This book is similar to an athlete's goal of scoring a personal best. The highest high jump. A perfect ten on a dive. 100% free throw percentage. Remember when the four-minute mile was considered impossible? Now the goal is 3:40! As soon as the four-minute mile was run, a new goal was set. Once a school is just where you want it, you should be itching to make it better.

I consider this book a trip on the road to excellence that leads to perfection. I also know that any system that is run by humans, for humans, and supported by humans, is excluded from reaching perfection, for obvious reasons. So the goal of this book is to share some of the ingredients that we feel are essential to seeking perfection, essential to developing excellence, and essential to the ultimate goal of most administrators—to provide the very best educational opportunities for kids.

If perfection is an unattainable goal, why write a book about it?

Jim Burgett: Excellence is attainable. Excellence is necessary for perfection. To achieve perfection, we have to attain excellence. Thus, this is a collection of what we see as foundations of excellence.

I guess the same question could be asked to the authors of the federal mandate No Child Left Behind. One of the main components of that law is that by a certain year every child will reach a specific level of academic achievement. Is this possible? Absolutely not. There isn't a sane educator in the world who thinks for one minute that every child will reach the same standard level of achievement. But the goal is worthy. The concept has merit. Over the years the rules and regulations have been tweaked and bent, twisted and revised, and they will continue to undergo overhauls, but in spite of all the talk and change, the road is still being traveled and the destination is still honorable. The same is true for this effort. We have tried to share what we feel are important elements in the quest for perfection, the quest for excellence. Again, it is the journey that is important.

Jim Rosborg: The goal of any organization always has to be to seek improvement. Strong leaders not only maintain current momentum in an organization, they seek to improve it. Seeking stability without efforts for positive change is the kiss of death for any school and its leaders. An effective leader takes good things and makes them better. This is why we wrote the book. We recognize that there are outstanding school leaders throughout this nation. Our goal is to make your school more effective on its way to attempting to achieve perfection.

Max McGee: As with any goal, the journey is always far more important and rewarding than the end result. As you strive to fashion the perfect school you learn more than you thought possible, become immersed in countless inspirational experiences, and see people differently. Though you will never have the perfect school, your efforts to create it will change your life, and the lives of those you touch, for the better.

In your May 2005 interview[2] on the *Audio Journal* each of you linked perfection to current school changes. Can you share and summarize some of those thoughts here?

Max McGee: Leadership is about change, and change is the only way to realize the perfect school. We know that change is not a matter of will or charisma, but requires inspiration, perspiration, motivation, and imagination. In describing the perfect principal, I focus on what he or she does to improve teaching and learning to assure that each child is taught the way he learns best and to create

---

[2] For a full text transcript of the program, see www.superintendents-and-principals.com.

a culture of growth where children and adults flourish. In discussing the perfect teachers and parents, I do not describe Our Miss Brooks or Jaime Escalante. I talk about growth and change, about the development of mind, body, and spirit in adults and the children they serve. Achieving perfection is about the courage, the will, and the action to set goals, to strive to achieve them, and to move a little bit further from here to there each day.

Jim Burgett: The *Audio Journal* interview asked a lot of questions about the only sure thing in education—change. During the interview each of the three authors shared some insight into areas that we thought were important for administrators as they strived to make a difference for kids. I talked about three basic skills that administrators need to continuously develop: how to work with legislators, being a model of ethical behavior, and communications. Each of these issues relates to the ever changing parameters of education.

A huge percentage of the changes we deal with in education come from our legislators. They may deal with funding (or lack of), special education laws, curricular mandates, required assessments, or something as mundane as what kind of sodas you can sell. The changes can range from your basic operational abilities to the numbering on the side of the buses.

The administrator who wants to be proactive, be a mover and player, needs to develop certain skills. Those skills include, but are not restricted to, being savvy about what is happening, reading legislative updates and journals, attending conferences and meetings, knowing the legislative process, and being proficient in communicating with legislators. If you want to pursue excellence, you have to have an understanding of the processes that mold our ability to deliver services, and you have to know how to be influential with the controlling powers.

Often lost in the discussion of administrative skills is ethical leadership. How to respond to ethical and political decision making. How to be a trusted leader and role model. How to make the right decisions for the right reasons. How to understand your own values and stick with them. How to be an exceptional, fair, and worthy community leader. There are processes to follow and checklists to mark that can help. These skills don't come with certification; they are learned. Excellent schools, as we so often state in the book, are built by excellent employees. To have an excellent school, you need to have an excellent staff. And that means they need to understand and cultivate excellence. The direction for this comes from strong and ethical leaders.

Finally, and very important, is the skill of communication. The road to excellence is a road that is easily understood; it's simple, clear, honest, and well defined. The trip to perfection is much safer and faster without potholes along the way. Potholes come from miscommunication, repeating information, confusing instructions, unclear procedures, and general confusion. Communicate a goal clearly, garnish understanding and support, work directly and honestly, and you arrive at your destination quicker and with greater enthusiasm. Make people understand, feel good, and appreciate what is going on and you will make giant strides toward an attitude of excellence. Effective communication skills are learned. Changes become easier to understand and respond to when they are appropriately defined and explained. Of all the skills that can make or break an administrator, communications could possibly be the most important.

Jim Rosborg: The perfect school has to start out with a common mission, a common set of goals and objectives, plus measurable outcomes that are evaluated for school improvement. Schools have to look at their leadership, have a strategic plan in place, have a faculty hiring plan to maximize instruction, and use a collaborative leadership style. There must be a positive institutional focus on helping employees maximize student performance. The students are the center of all goals. The perfect school knows this shared vision is a necessity to the school's and student's success. The perfect school is going to take the information available, then analyze and evaluate it to see how successful the product is. In schools, the main product is student performance. The main goal is to help the student become a successful citizen.

As we stated earlier, change is an ongoing part of the educational process. In the May, 2005 interview with the *Audio Journal*, I stated: "Don't be afraid to admit that you don't know everything." In your quest for perfection, you will make mistakes. The best thing to minimize those mistakes is to collaborate with colleagues and key stakeholders. Get a mentor. In fact, one of our hopes with *The Perfect School* is that we can be a mentor to you and your thought process. Find that person you can work with: someone to whom you can ask questions, someone you can trust, someone you can use for support. I think that is imperative to seeking perfection. A great educator is a better assimilator of ideas than innovator.

With change there will be conflict. Your job is to provide solutions to the conflicts. This is sometimes hard to do. There are always going to be situations where two employees argue with each other, and you have to make the decision. The decision you make is going to upset at least one of the two. The best decision comes from the answer to this question, "What is best for kids?" That will help you better deal with conflict and change and be consistent with your decisions.

Finally, you have to show a good work ethic. Your staff has to know that you are going to be with them in anything they do as long as it is best for kids. If we expect teachers and other staff members to work hard, we have to work harder while taking every opportunity to congratulate them for their successes. The main focus of leadership has to be to help the teacher be more successful in the classroom, which leads to greater student success in the classroom. Without successful teachers, the perfect school is impossible to even strive for, much less achieve.

Can you summarize in a sentence or so the most important principle or guideline to seek perfection that you found for each of the chapters you wrote for this book?

Jim Burgett: The goal of perfection is based on excellence. My focus in *The Perfect School* centers on four concepts: service, character, perception, and quality.

Schools are service providers to all their stakeholders. Yet service comes in all sizes and shapes. The only service that really matters is good service, but I propose that schools seek a level of outstanding, second-to-none, truly superb quality service. I share how this mindset can be developed.

Service reflects the general character of the system, and for that reason we discuss character education. When someone hears the term "character education" they usually think of a program devised for elementary students. That's okay, but that is not what I mean. I am talking about developing character throughout the system. Not just by students, but by all participants. Well defined values and expected levels of character result in a quality system, a system that wants to provide quality service and exceptional learning opportunities.

Perception is the picture someone paints in their mind when they see or experience something. Often it's a valid reflection of the situation, but sometimes it's far from it. Thus perception may or may not reflect reality, but to the observer, if they don't know anything different, what they see is real. For this reason it is imperative that schools strive to honestly communicate and demonstrate the very best they can. The fewer the concerns, the better the quality. This chapter talks about how to realize and repair perception.

Finally, we talk about quality. The perfect school does not depend on walnut paneling or reflecting ponds in the yard. It depends on people—the higher the quality of people, the better the perception; the better the character, the better the service. In fact, everything depends on the quality of the staff. Building a high quality staff is not a short-term goal, but rather a long-term business. This chapter talks about eliminating the weakest links and replacing them with the highest quality.

Jim Rosborg: In my chapters I will deal with major federal impactors such as *A Nation at Risk*, Individual with Disabilities Education Act, the No Child Left Behind Act, and Title One Reading and Mathematics Act. How can we take these major curricular and school finance acts and use their ideas to attain the perfect school? How can we use assessment that centers around these mandates? How can we bridge current educational gaps? How can we present results in a positive light? What changes are needed in the current curricular structures to improve student learning? By continually asking what is best for the student, the results of these actions can lead to giant steps towards perfection.

Max McGee: In this book I describe perfect parents, perfect teachers and staff, and perfect principals. Actually, as Mary Poppins describes herself, they are "practically perfect in every way." Though they may not be able to slide up the banister, keep the brattiest kids in line, or sing in tune, perfect parents, teachers, and staff, plus practically perfect principals, are essential to the perfect school. No matter how "perfect" the building looks or how comprehensive the curriculum may be, without adults all working together to assure that every child learns and grows to achieve unrealized, untapped potential, the school will remain mediocre.

The guiding principle of the perfect school, then, is that schools are about people—the adult people who make a daily difference in the lives of children—who need to be at their best pretty much all the time.

Is it a waste of time to read about perfection in a school?

Jim Rosborg: The worst waste of time for a leader is not to define the ideal first (like perfection) before seeking improvements that imply its realization. Effective leaders reflect on their current and previous learning in their role as a student, parent, and educator. In this reflection, leaders determine where they are in the present and what methods they are going to use for improvements in the future. That is what we do in this book. We ask where we are, then we take you where we think schools should be in the future on that path toward perfection. If you get one idea out of this book to improve your school, then this book has *not* been a waste of time. We feel that we will provide you with many ideas and stimulate your thinking so that many more great ideas will evolve in your school to help students becoming successful citizens.

Jim Burgett: The honest answer to this question is yes. It is a waste of time to read about perfection if you don't plan to utilize what you read. I guess it would be like buying a book that tells you how to grow award-winning tomatoes and then never buying the seeds. I suppose you could dream of big, luscious, tasty tomatoes—just like you could dream of a top-notch school system—but to me that would indeed be just a waste of time and talent.

The goal of this book is to inspire its readers to take action. The three of us have been moderately successful administrators. We have helped our schools receive awards, and we have been recognized a time or two for our own leadership skills. But the real reason we wrote this book is our passion to make a difference. We think we know what it takes to move a district from good to outstanding. We believe it is possible to travel the road of excellence and strive for perfection. We also believe that if the reader only implements the concepts in one or two chapters of this book, they will still improve the quality of their school or system. The waste would be to read about perfection, have the passion to make a difference, and then do nothing.

Max McGee: Yes it is … if you have nothing to do with schools, education, or tax paying. For the rest of it, reading about the perfect school matters a lot for the quality of education in our schools. The most important people in education today are not in Washington, your state capital, or the school office. They are in our classrooms, ready to learn something—hopefully what we are trying to teach them. What they learn and what they become depends on our ability to create as perfect a school as possible for each child, even accepting that the perfect school for Joe will likely be different than the one for Jane. This book will not help you create a perfect school but it will help you contribute to making your school a little more perfect for its students, the leaders of tomorrow.

Chapter Two

The Perfect Teacher
and Perfect Staff

Max McGee

The perfect school has perfect teachers and perfect support staff. These perfect professionals are distinguished by several qualities and characteristics. They (1) build a close personal relationship with each child, (2) are "with it," (3) move each child from "here to there" every day, (4) teach the way the kids learn instead of forcing kids to learn the way they teach, (5) hold the highest expectations for all students, (6) make each day special for each student, (7) give each child a voice and assist in the development of their identity, (8) let no one fail, (9) have an insatiable thirst for knowing more and the drive to be innovative and creative, and (10) make valuable contributions beyond the classroom walls.

"Joey has a real joy of life that he demonstrates each day," wrote Mrs. B. on our son's first grade report card. Though I had been in education for 25 years, I really didn't know if that was a good or a bad comment. What I did know was that it was accurate. Though she had only known him a few months, she had captured the essence of our junior Jimmy Buffet.

She was the perfect teacher for Joey. Her classroom was highly structured. She wasn't about to let anybody leave her first grade without learning to read. And though she appreciated how charming our son could be, she was one of the few teachers who caught on early that he could talk his way out of hard work. She kept him on task.

Throughout school Joey has thrived with structure and floundered without it. Though we never thought he had any particular mathematical talent, his high school teacher, Mrs. C., brought it out of him. Every assignment for the quarter was posted, he had his grade updated every week, and she challenged him to solve tougher problems, giving him the principles, concepts, and confidence to thrive.

As perfect as Mrs. B. and Mrs. C. were for Joey, they would not have been the perfect teacher for our older son. Born strong willed, he approached every structured environment determined to reshape it to his needs. As he grew up, we encountered a new "fort" nearly every week as he arranged his room, the basement, the garage, anything that could be moved into some new, incredible structure. Throughout school, we knew within the first day or two of the semester whether he was going to get an A, a B, or a gentleman's D. Structure and authority were invitations to rebel.

So who were his perfect teachers? Mrs. A and Ms. F. Realizing Mike was basically a non-reader after first grade, his second grade teacher Mrs. A also realized that she had to build a nurturing, caring relationship with him, then give him plenty of attention as well to let him make mistakes so he'd keep working until he got it right. She not only taught him to read, she also helped him appreciate talents that his other teachers found threatening. She loved his creativity, his ability to build, create, and draw—even his swagger. Unlike so many teachers, she accepted and strengthened his boyness rather than seeing it as a detriment or an impediment to learning.

In high school, Ms. F., his work-study teacher, was quick to realize that he had enormous mechanical talents. Despite sizeable bureaucratic obstacles, she found a way for him to earn credits taking auto mechanics classes at local community colleges. During finals week, instead of subjecting him to both the stress of final exams and temptations to party, she arranged a weeklong internship with an auto dealer in southern Illinois.

In addition to these experiences with my own children, as a teacher, principal, and superintendent I have known several "perfect teachers." As Chairman of the Golden Apple Foundation, I have the honor of presenting Golden Apples, our "Academy Awards" of teaching, to the top ten teachers in Chicago every year. This televised production shows why they are the perfect teachers—they know each child and treat them as their own, they have the highest expectations and do not let anyone fail, they make learning lively, they make contributions far beyond their class-room walls, and, above all, they are humbled by the responsibility of their jobs and each student's gifts. Noted one winner, "As a teacher it didn't take me long to realize that although I was the oldest person in the room, I wasn't the smartest person in the room."

Even the Golden Apple teachers, however, have their detractors, and even the most marginal teachers have devoted students and parents who are number one fans. As with the "practically perfect principal," there is no perfect teacher for every child. There are, however, as illustrated above, certain qualities that the very best teachers share.

In this chapter we will explore what makes the perfect teacher. We'll also go beyond that to discuss what makes the perfect professional staff in the perfect school and what school leaders can do to help every professional become their very best.

Perfect Professionals?

As superintendents we learned long ago that great schools are only as great as the three Ps: principals, parents, and professionals. As much as we would like to think that we had something to do with test scores increasing, drop-out rates decreasing, attitudes improving, and suspensions declining, we know full well that we do not teach the kids. That is the job of professionals during school hours and parents the rest of the time. Others have written eloquently about "the right people on the bus" and we have our own book-shelves and film libraries full of perfect teachers, from Jaime Escalante, whose exceptional accomplishments were featured in the film *Stand and Deliver,* to Erin Gruwell of *Freedom Writers* fame. Rather than inundate you with other examples of perfect teachers—and we have lots of them—we are going to share what the perfect professionals as a whole bring to the perfect school.

We want to emphasize that when we talk about perfect professionals we are not only talking about perfect teachers. Professionals include the bus drivers, the teacher assistants, the clerical staff, the receptionist, the nurse, the lunch servers, the custodians, the tech crew, the maintenance engineers, and anyone and everyone who is paid to support the operation of the perfect school. We consider them professionals and teachers.

They are teachers because, as we all know, children learn best by example. From the bus driver they learn courtesy and how to mediate conflict; from the custodian they learn about pride in taking care of a room or a building and the value of hard work; from the one-on-one assistants they learn how to work with the severely disabled, and from the school secretary they learn how to do twelve things at once—in modern jargon, to "multi-task." Though not reading, writing, or arithmetic, the lessons learned from the support staff serve our students equally as well throughout life.

We also consider the support staff to be professionals because they are paid not just to work six to eight hours a day but to put their heart and soul into their work. At the perfect school they are treated like professionals and in turn are expected to look and behave like professionals.

If you ever doubt the powerful influence of these professionals in students' lives, we double dog dare you to outsource their services. Though we and our peers have done it and lived to lead another day, we realized that nothing incurs parental anxiety, staff acrimony, and student unrest more than replacing the familiar faces of the custodians, bus drivers, and lunch staff they see every day with employees from a "faceless" outside organization. In all fairness to outside service providers, many of these companies have high professional standards and in time their staff develops the same positive relationships with students, teachers, and parents. The transition, however, is hell, especially if your culture embraces all staff members as true professionals in educating the whole child.

What the Perfect Teacher Does

When we ask folks to describe the perfect teacher, they always think of the best teacher they ever had and talk about him or her— or they describe the most recent film teacher, like Erin Gruwell, powerfully portrayed by Hillary Swank in *Freedom Writers*. But when we ask this question, we have never, ever had anyone give us a "composite" of a perfect teacher, e.g. "The perfect teacher has Ms. A's personality, Mr. B's structure, Mrs. C's sense of humor, and Dr. D's incredible knowledge." The perfect teacher is not a collection of characteristics but first and foremost a human being. What we have learned from asking this question, reflecting on our own perfect teachers and watching those perfect teachers we have been blessed to employ, is what they share in common. So, rather than citing scholarly research that supports what follows, please indulge your authors as we share our observations of those unique traits as we have seen them during the 100+ years we have spent in classrooms!

Perfect teachers build a close personal relationship with each child. The best teachers know what is special about every student they teach. They know their likes and dislikes, their friends and enemies, their hopes and dreams, and their worries and fears. They talk with, not at, them as close friends. They know how they learn best and their special talents. They know the weaknesses and the opportunities they present. They know how to praise and discipline beyond "good job" and "keep your hands to yourself." They share their lives with their students, and their students know the name of their pets, their special hobbies, and their own special talents. They share their special experiences from travel to graduate school to their favorite books and movies. They give each child a voice and help every young man and young woman realize and develop his or her individual identity.

They are "with it." Actually, some research supports our contention that the quality of "with-it-ness" distinguishes the best teachers. It is as impossible to describe "with-it-ness" as it is to describe good jazz, but you know it when you hear (or see) it. "With-it-ness" is the antithesis of "clueless." Just ask students. They will tell you which teachers "get it" and which don't. Teachers who are "with it" understand the subculture of the classroom as well as the larger context of their students. They know and appreciate—or at least tolerate—the latest "fashion," even if it includes wearing pants so low that boxer shorts hang out and earrings the size of hula hoops. Teachers don't demonstrate "with-it-ness" by how they dress; some of the most "with it" teachers we know wear ties or skirts every day. They demonstrate it by knowing what is going on all the time. They realize a girl's hair flip or raised eyebrow can be as devastating to a female peer as a karate chop, and they "get" that for many young men school is a small part in a big day of exerting maleness and fitting into a subculture of peers. "With it" teachers make the most of "teachable moments," whether using a current event, something that happened at lunch, a neighborhood conflict, or an unexpected classroom experience to teach about life. Though committed to teaching the curriculum, we find "with it" teachers put more emphasis on students than standards and they teach kids, not classes.

They move each child from "here to there" every day. Perfect teachers make sure that kids learn. They make the most of every minute in the classroom. Transitions from one activity to another are in seconds, not minutes. When students leave the class at the end of the period or at the end of the day, they know more than when they walked in the door. The perfect teacher may not even keep lesson plans, but he or she begins each hour and each day with a clear purpose and commitment to make sure that each child learns something new.

When kids don't learn from the way they teach, they teach the way the kids learn. If we had a nickel for every time we heard teachers complain about how kids just can't learn, we would have gathered enough money to give our books away. When students get Cs, Ds, or worse, many teachers first blame the student. We contend they should look in the mirror. We agree with the late Benjamin Bloom that all students are capable of receiving As and Bs. Perfect teachers may or may not use Bloom's taxonomy when they teach,[1] but what they do better than most teachers is quickly figure out how each student learns best and then teach to that style. They excel at differentiating instruction to challenge every child and spend the most time with the neediest students. The key point: none of their students fail—they find a way to reach each one.

They hold the highest expectations for all students. The perfect teacher expects every child to succeed and excel no matter what type of home life they have. They provide the support for each child to overcome the problems they face outside of school. They really believe that each child has enormous, untapped potential and that with the right teaching, he or she can achieve what others never thought they could. I was recently invited to give a keynote

---

[1] Bloom, B., *Taxonomy of Educational Objectives. Handbook 1*. New York: Longman, 1956.

address on closing the achievement gap and was also asked to provide some ideas for a luncheon speaker that same day. I immediately thought of a perfect principal and some perfect teachers I had seen in a "Golden Spike" school that had, in fact, closed the gap for several years. Of all the speakers throughout the day, me included, they were hands down the best; they also received the longest and loudest applause. Here was their message: "We are responsible for student achievement. When a child fails, it is our responsibility. Children come to us with a great deal of baggage. We set that aside and teach them. If a child does not do well in our classroom, we reevaluate our teaching rather than make excuses. We never give up!"

They make each day special for each student. How many times do you hear someone say, "You made my day!"? Not often, but think how special you do feel when someone like a student, colleague, family member, or even boss says that to you or actually does "make your day." The perfect teacher more often than not strives to "make their day" for every student, plus the day of many colleagues with whom he or she interacts. The perfect teacher revels in seeing people "light up" when they make a comment, send a note, provide a special touch, recognize an accomplishment, or do something else that may well be the most important thing they remember at the end of that day.

They let no one fail. The idea that perfect teachers do not let children fail has been mentioned earlier and will be mentioned again. It is such a distinguishing characteristic of and so common among perfect teachers that we cannot repeat it enough. Perfect teachers refuse to allow students to languish. They fight to reach every child and they never give up no matter how hard the student tries to have them give up on them. Failing students are what keep perfect teachers awake at night. They toss and turn and dream about students they can't reach, often waking up to write a note about an "aha" idea that might just work to engage the toughest of students. Those they can't reach stay with them for life. (To this day, I remember Sydney, Scott, and Ruby, whom I taught in 1972, because I simply could not "turn them on" to learning.)

They have a lot of fun at work. How common are complaints about "low morale." (As superintendents, we have even been accused of contributing to low morale or supporting principals or parents who drove morale to its lowest point. That hurts.) What is interesting, however, is that we do not hear these complaints from perfect teachers. They realize that every individual is responsible for his or her own morale and someone cannot make you feel good or bad—you choose how you feel. Though perfect teachers also have times of low and high morale, that is usually tied to how they are impacting the lives of their students or how they are dealing with life outside of school. To keep their own morale high, they find ways to make days at work a lot of fun. They enjoy being with their students and seldom does a class go by without a few good laughs. The perfect teacher also makes the school more fun by being there. They find ways to help others manage the high stress and to contribute to a positive climate.

They have an insatiable thirst for knowing more. Perfect teachers realize that they are not perfect. They understand that they can learn much from reading, attending classes and workshops, and talking with other teachers. They strive for perfection and walk the talk of "lifelong learning." Perfect teachers, though among the best in their schools, strive for National Board Certification; without exception, once they attain it, they admit that they still have a lot to learn. They are eager to learn more and engage in professional development activities.

They make countless contributions beyond the classroom walls. The perfect teacher is not one to focus solely on his or her students. There is no doubt that most of his attention is devoted to the children he serves, but as a perfect teacher, he realizes a responsibility to a "greater good," be it improving the department, strengthening the school, upgrading the district's quality, or having an impact on colleagues in other districts. Perfect teachers are "doers." They relish conversations about education and contribute innovative ideas to their departments. They actively participate in developing and implementing school improvement plans and/or find leadership roles in district curriculum development or strategic planning. They lead book clubs and study groups or bring in an article to share with colleagues. Some find a way to share their insights and expertise through publishing articles and making presentations at regional, state, and national conferences. The perfect teacher strives to make his school or district and the profession better places for students and staff.

The Perfect Staff

Of course all of the above is also true for support staff, and we have plenty of examples to share.

A perfect staff builds a close personal relationship with each child. Every school day the bus driver is the first employee to meet and greet most students. The driver has the potential to get the students' day off to a great start or to start them off on the wrong foot. Balancing structured rules for a safe ride with humor, greetings, and an understanding of every student is difficult but is something the perfect bus drivers do as second nature. They know their riders as people and they often know the families too. They interact with the students as they come on the bus, talking about their sports, their musical instruments, their classes, their families, and current or special events. In our districts, our top drivers and crossing guards are regularly found in pictures taken the first day of school, and they receive lots of gifts at Christmastime.

They are "with it." The perfect school secretaries and assistants are generally the most "with it" people we know. Not only do they know all of the students' and parents' names, they also know the parents who need TLC and reassurance, they keep the "helicopters" (parents who cannot stop hovering over their children) at a safe distance, and they provide immediate access to those few who get the direct line to the principal. When a child appears at her desk midday complaining of stomachache, the perfect assistant intuitively knows if it is due to a test, lunch, a playground tussle, or real sickness. High intuition is a sure sign of "with-it-ness."

They move each child from "here to there" every day. One-to-one special education assistants are our heroes. Working with students who have the most serious needs, they patiently persist in helping their charges make minute, incremental progress and celebrate every gain, no matter how small. "Inclusion" and, more recently, "response to intervention (RTI)" have been credited for the success we have seen in helping our special education students, but it is less about the concept and more about the people, our special education assistants, who have enabled these children to be included.

When kids don't learn the way they teach, they teach the way the kids learn. Today it's not uncommon to see more than one adult in a classroom. Whereas an "extra pair of hands" used to be a clerical assistant running—we are dating ourselves here—dittos and grading papers, the classroom assistants now help individual students, provide small group instruction, and consult with the teacher on the best way to reach the student. Examples might be helping a young girl "get" a math problem by explaining it in a different way or assisting a young boy on how to write a paragraph instead of a sentence.

They hold high expectations for all students. My favorite example is Lionel, the retired custodian of Harper School. Under his watchful eye and hard work, the school literally sparkled every day. The real key to his success, however, was that he knew each of the 450 students by name, and by his example, good humor, and an occasional stern look, he instilled a sense of pride in the students for the school. They were the first to pick up stray trash in the halls, remove litter from the playground, and even wipe their feet because they loved and respected him.

They let no one fail. Actually, they let no school fail. The perfect building engineers do whatever it takes to get school open and running despite enormous challenges of nasty weather, old boilers, and large-scale power failures. I was most recently reminded of this during a whopper blizzard. In the upper Midwest, superintendents have the unenviable responsibility of deciding when to call a "snow day." Being a hands-on kind of guy, on the night of the raging storm I left my home at 3:00 a.m. to drive 30 miles to the office. I arrived at 4:30 thinking I would be the first in the building and would need to shovel the first path for the staff. Our head engineer, however, had beat me in by an hour and already had his crew clearing sidewalks in front of the schools and plowing the parking lots. At some personal risk, Stan and his team had braved the bad roads because of their commitment to our kids.

They have fun. When was the last time Harry Potter dished you up a bowl of soup, Viola Swamp flipped your grilled cheese, or Sarah Plain and Tall counted your change on the lunch line? A far cry from the "blue ladies" who served permanent scowls along with our lunches when we were in high school, we have seen our cafeteria workers make an institutional lunch more like a family picnic. They dress up as book characters, run contests, and play music so that lunch hour becomes a pleasant interlude during the day. Most importantly, they talk with students and know them by name.

They have an insatiable thirst for knowing more. The perfect support staff is always looking for ways to help the teachers, the school, and the district. The most recent example came when we recently overhauled our tech staff. Our former "techies" were seemingly burdened by every request, complained about "ignorant" teachers and administrators who did not know a WAN from a LAN, and went out of their way to make the simplest repair a major undertaking. Our new crew chose a whole new attitude. They actually visit schools, teach staff how to do their own trouble shooting and simple repairs, dress professionally, and go out of their way to find ways to prevent problems before they happen.

They make countless contributions beyond the classroom walls. The perfect support staff members participate on SIP teams, take professional development classes, and volunteer for committee work. Including them, we frequently find that their insights help everyone make better decisions for children, the school, and the community.

We are certain each of you could relate similar examples of perfect professionals—both teachers and support staff—from your schools and districts. The challenge for leaders is to have a critical mass of these perfect professionals. To do so, we have two responsibilities: (1) to create a culture where commitment to perfection grows and flourishes, and (2) to identify, inspire, motivate, and nurture individuals to exceed their potential. Let's turn to some ideas for stepping up to this challenge.

The Perfect Professional Culture

As we said at the outset, the perfect school is far more than a collection of perfect individuals. On the contrary, a school with 99%

perfect professionals may be a long, long way from being the perfect school. In fact, we contend that to have anything approaching it, you must create a perfect professional culture, that is, a common commitment to what I call Common Core Beliefs, and to making professional development a collective mission and not an individual endeavor.

Common Core Beliefs

High expectations. Every staff member believes and articulates nothing less than the highest expectations for every individual child and the entire student body. They know that what children can do almost always exceeds what others have pegged as their "potential."

Efficacy. Each staff member believes that he or she is responsible and accountable for what children learn, despite the circumstances. Recall the quote from the Golden Spike top teachers earlier in this chapter. They realized that no matter what "baggage" or burden a child carries, the teacher can overcome it. In affluent schools, teachers too often believe that children will succeed anyway because of genes, successful parents, and financial resources. It is well documented in research and practice, however, that when teachers take responsibility for children, even the brightest and most advantaged children can exceed their supposed potential.

Teaching the way children learn. While we admire and support the work of the many authors who research, write, and teach about differentiation of instruction, we contend that when a school culture follows the simple premise "if they don't learn the way we teach, then we have to teach the way children learn," achievement and self-esteem soar.

Parents are partners. This is a core belief of perfect schools, and it is demonstrated every day. Teachers find ways to communicate regularly, or even more frequently, through calls, e-mail, newsletters, and even personal home visits. Parents report feeling welcome in the school and while embraced as partners they are also given specific responsibilities to help their students. Teachers respect parents and are comfortable having them in their room and the school. They talk with them and realize that, like teaching, parenting is hard work and more art than science.

Professional Development

Many less than perfect schools spend a great deal of time and money on professional development. Many teachers get tuition reimbursement for courses they take and workshops they attend. Others receive stipends for researching the latest developments in curriculum and instruction. Still others read an article, hear a speech, get an idea from a colleague, or attend an in-house class taught by a peer. While these are all beneficial to the individual teacher and perhaps to his or her students, they do very little to improve the school as a whole, to move it from good to great and great to greater, or create the common culture found in a perfect school.

Here is our take on the power of professional development.

Common goals v. individual pursuits. Too often, professional development is left to the discretion of individual staff. Although their learning may help improve their teaching for their class of 25 students (or classes of 150), the teacher the students have next year or even next period will not likely have made similar changes to their teaching. On the contrary, in the perfect school professional development is closely tied to collaboratively developing school-wide goals, and the "community of learners" has common professional development experiences through workshops, video, peer coaching, study groups, book clubs, and the like. Consequently, from period to period, teacher to teacher, grade to grade, and year to year, students benefit from teachers with deep shared knowledge and common commitment.

Respect for and learning from the best teachers. The best teachers are often the most modest and do not like to stand out. In too many schools, they face considerable peer pressure not to be too good and not to do too much extra because it "makes us all look bad" or goes beyond what the teacher contract prescribes. In some schools, the best teachers are even ostracized or ridiculed. With such great pressure to regress to the mean, it is no surprise then that the best teachers would just as soon close their doors and work with their classes. In the high-poverty, high-performing schools as well as in other perfect schools, the best teachers are revered. They are also asked to share demonstration lessons at faculty meetings, mentor new teachers, and coach veterans. People seek advice from them and they lead in-house workshops or classes.

Engagement in "critical conversations." Learning doesn't happen without discourse. As Walter Lippman said, "Where all think alike, no one thinks very much."[2] The culture of most schools features unanimous agreements and an air of "niceness." While we think being nice counts for a lot, we also know that in perfect schools teachers understand that they have a voice and are encouraged to hold what Susan Scott calls "fierce conversations,"[3] which are meaningful and sometimes heated discussions around teaching and learning, school goals, and even ways to reach a particular child. Teachers are free to challenge the thinking of one another and the administration through conversation and dialogue without fear because mutual respect is the cornerstone of the school. Too many schools follow Dr. Jerry Harvey's "Road to Abilene,"[4] where everyone goes in the same direction—the wrong one—because they don't want to disagree or rock the boat. Can you imagine how different our U.S. Constitution would have looked if the Founding Fathers had all politely agreed instead of debating and fighting for core principles? Can you imagine how different the perfect school looks when thinking and conversation are respected in contrast to most schools where everyone goes along just to go along? The difference of night and day…

[2] Lippman, W., *Public Opinion*. New York: Simon and Schuster, 1922. .
[3] Scott, Susan., *Fierce Conversations: Achieving Success in Life and at Work One Conversation at a Time*. New York: The Berkley Publishing, Group, 2002.
[4] Harvey, J.B., *The Abilene Paradox and Other Meditations on Management*. New York: Wiley and Sons, 1996.

Perfection is Made, not Born

A huge, important question remains—how do I get perfect professionals to and in my school? What's needed is a website called www.perfectprofessionals.com, a 1-800-FORKIDS free phone, or a teacher preparation institute like Withitness State University! Alas, you aren't going to find many self-labeled perfect professionals on the job market, and if they are out there, your standardized interview questions and screening processes won't be able to identify them. You may find a few by networking with colleagues or even pillaging your neighboring districts, but most likely you will need to grow your own.

Fortunately, perfect professionals are made, not born. So what can you do? In addition to reading my chapter called "Perfect Principals," here are a few of Mother McGee's helpful hints for actions you can take that will create an environment where teachers and support staff can become perfect professionals, where perfect professionals will want to be, and where they will remain.

Know them as people. Perfect teachers have close relationships with their students, and perfect leaders have close relationships with their staff. This doesn't mean that they have to socialize with the teachers every Friday night or take them to lunch once a month. Rather, building a close relationship means knowing their names, their passions, and their concerns. Pay sincere concern to their interests, whether it's their family, their health, or their personal goals such as running a marathon, gardening, or my current favorite, not missing an episode of *24*. When passing in the hall, stopping in a class, or buzzing in and out of the lounge, a few quick comments that reflect both personal and professional interest go a long way. "Linda, so how is your son Patrick doing at Notre Dame this year?"; "I can't wait to see the first bouquet from your garden, Jane!", and "Good luck in your race this weekend, Randy" are more than just pleasantries, they show that the people who work for you matter to you.

Articulate clear expectations, direction, vision, and goals. We all know that teachers and staff want a leader who assures that the perfect school runs smoothly, but if you get down to what they really want in a leader, it is more about clear vision and direction for the school. Teachers want to know what expectations their leaders have for them. We have found that the best leaders readily share these and, from their vision and expectations, work with teachers to derive clear, specific, measurable goals for the school and for each staff member.

Demonstrate reciprocal accountability. In this era of account-ability, more than water flows downhill. The standard accountabil-ity model is based on a relationship where superintendents are ac-countable to Boards, principals are accountable to superintendents, and teachers to principals. In the school system, middle school is accountable to high school, elementary to middle school, etc. You get the idea—if you are a pre-school teacher, then it's all your fault! (I'm joking, of course. Pre-school teachers, in our opinion, should get paid more, or at least as well as, the most talented high school teacher.) We are not joking, however, that in the perfect school accountability flows uphill. A real leader is one who is ac-countable to and takes responsibility for his or her teachers and most importantly realizes that the success of the school is the hands of the teacher so he or she must be accountable to them and provide the support, resources, and climate necessary for them to excel.

Richard Elmore[5] and Jim Collins,[6] two top authors, have writ-ten eloquently about reciprocal accountability, and we share their views. Notes Elmore, "Accountability must be a reciprocal proc-ess. For every increment of performance I demand from you, I have an equal responsibility to provide you with the capacity to meet that expectation. Likewise, for every investment you make in my skill and knowledge, I have a reciprocal responsibility to dem-onstrate some new increment in performance. This is the principle of 'reciprocity of accountability for capacity'." Collins explains that the Level Five leader, "looks out the window, not in the mir-ror, to apportion credit for the success of the company—to other people, external factors, and good luck—and looks in the mirror, not out the window, to apportion responsibility for poor results,

---

[5] Elmore, R., *Bridging the Gap Between Standards and Achievement: The Imperative for Professional Development in Education*. Washing-ton, D.C.: Albert Shanker Institute, 2002.
[6] Collins, J., *Good to Great: Why Some Companies Make the Leap and Others Don't*. New York: Harper Collins, 2001.

never blaming other people, external factors, or bad luck."[7] In the perfect school, the leader is the most accountable individual and assures that the staff, the parents, and the central office realize that he or she is the one responsible when things go wrong.

Respect, recognize, and reinforce their success and strong effort. Leaders who want to develop the perfect school find ways to show staff members they are appreciated and to reinforce excellent teaching. We believe that a hand-written note is the most effective way, but even a personal e-mail, a surprise token gift, or just a face-to-face thanks all work well, too. Generally, teachers appreciate these efforts more than recognition at a staff or Board meeting, which are best for the recognition of groups or teams. Another important method of respecting and rewarding teachers is to include them. Take them to a conference, send a small group to a workshop (preferably to somewhere really nice), make them part of a team that gives a presentation to the Board or community, or have them meet with an important guest. This type of professional recognition literally shows the staff how professional you believe they are.

Lead by example. Though it should go without saying, we must say it: People want to work for a boss who is courageous yet calm, tough on the problem and easy on people, and strong yet sensitive. They want to see someone who exhibits class, grace, and composure under fire. They expect the leader to be a presence, the face of the school, and to have energy, heart, enthusiasm, and a darn good sense of humor. Actions do speak louder than words, so it is more important for the leader to lead by example than to tell people about his or her leadership style.

Thrust greatness upon them. Shakespeare wrote, "Be not afraid of greatness: some are born great, some achieve greatness and some have greatness thrust upon them."[8] To foster a culture for perfect professionals, the best leaders find ways to thrust greatness on the professional staff by giving them the opportunity to demonstrate leadership beyond classroom walls, such as having them

---

[7] Elmore, R., ***Building a New Structure for School Leadership***. Washington D.C.: The Shanker Institute, 2000.
[8] Shakespeare, W., *Twelfth Night*, Act II, Scene V.

take leadership roles in creating prairie gardens and outdoor class-rooms, running book clubs, chairing curriculum mapping teams, planning strategic action committees, and leading intervention teams that identify ways to help non-IEP students from falling through the cracks.

Summary

Perfect professionals include teachers and support staff because everyone teaches students in some way every day. Perfect professionals share several commonalities, including:

- They build a close personal relationship with each child.
- They are "with it."
- They move each child from "here to there" every day.
- When kids don't learn the way they teach, they teach the way the kids learn.
- They hold the highest expectations for all students.
- They make each day special for each student.
- They give each child a voice and assist in the development of their identity.
- They let no one fail.
- They have an insatiable thirst for knowing more and the drive to be innovative and creative.
- They make valuable contributions beyond the classroom walls.

It takes more than a collection of "perfect professionals" to make a perfect school. The culture must support common commitment to vision, direction, and goals, and share core beliefs of the unlimited potential and the highest expectations for every child.

Finally, perfect professionals are hard to find. You actually have to help them realize their potential and provide opportunities, experiences, and a climate conducive to growth and expanding potential.

Chapter Three

The Perfect Parent

Max McGee

One cannot have a perfect school without perfect parents. Perfect parents are those who are (1) engaged in their child's education, (2) share high aspirations for their children with their children, and (3) provide resources and support necessary to help their children become independent learners. Perfect parents are made, not born, and school leaders can help and support parents by (1) communicating realistic expectations for engagement, (2) having written policies and established practices for engaging parents, and by (3) using innovative methods to reach all parents and caregivers.

The perfect school has perfect parents. These are not necessarily the mothers and fathers of the boys and girls of Lake Woebegone. Some perfect parents have children who aren't gifted or even above average. Some have children who stay up too late, eat too many "non-nutritional" snacks, and occasionally listen to inappropriate music. Some have girls who play with dolls and boys who play with trucks and some have boys who play with dolls and girls who play with trucks.

We three authors of this book are all parents who tried our best to be perfect parents. I don't know about Jim and Jim, but I was never a "perfect parent" by any conventional definition. When our Michael was very young, Jan and I decided that we would be the perfect parents. He would have trucks *and* dolls for toys, vegetables would be served at every meal, television would be limited to 30 minutes a day, music and art lessons would supplement baseball and basketball practices, we would read to him every night, and he would never have toy guns, knives, or swords. All went well for a few months, but when he turned three we realized the full futility of our efforts. Walking into preschool to pick him up one day, I was greeted with "Pow. Pow. Pow. I got you, Dad." In his hand was the state of Florida—a puzzle piece that his imagination had fashioned into a gun. Where did we go wrong?

After three children and one grandchild, plus an additional 20-some years around boys and girls, Jan and I have calmed down a lot and both have come to appreciate that we didn't go wrong. We know we should have been more impressed with his vivid imagination than shocked by being gunned down by Florida. Likewise, when we were still reading to him at bedtime when he was in seventh grade, we should not have been quite so upset when he asked us to put down whatever classic novel we had chosen and to read Steven King's *Christine* instead. *Christine*, yikes, that's so scary! I would never have been able to get to sleep, how could my son? Where did we go wrong? Looking back, we should have been celebrating that he still enjoyed having us read to him at bedtime.

I realize that as adults we have a lot of influence in our children's lives, but I have also come to appreciate how that influence balances with their innate personality, their "boyness" or "girlness," and the myriad of outside influences that touch them. As educators we know that this realization is key to assuring that each of "tomorrow's leaders" has the education they need to achieve their untapped academic potential and develop sound values and strong character.

Being humbled by our own children and our struggles as parents, we will limit our thoughts here about perfect parents to how parents relate with our schools. Underpinning this conversation is our core belief that we will not be able to help any child reach—or better yet, exceed—his or her potential without the support and love of a parent, grandparent, guardian, or other adult outside of school. Recent research on teaching and learning is replete with evidence that "high quality" teachers make the most difference in improving achievement. With all due respect to our colleagues engaged in teacher quality research, our gut tells us that without parents who support their children, communicate with the school, and work as educational partners, even the very best teacher would not succeed.

In fact, there is a growing body of research that shows parental engagement and home school partnerships significantly improve student achievement at all grade levels and across all backgrounds: "Research studies have consistently showed a relationship between parental involvement…and improved student achievement. This relationship holds across families of all economic, racial/ethnic, and educational backgrounds and for students of all ages."[1]

In this chapter, we will share a few characteristics of perfect parents, identify the key components of parent engagement, and offer a few ideas for creating a climate that will uncover the perfection in all parents.

Qualities of Perfect Parents

Perfect parents come in ones and twos, extra-larges and extra-smalls. Some are literally rocket scientists and others are, sadly, homeless. Some have a Ph. D. in English literature and others do not speak a word of English. Some perfect parents are not the parents of the students at all, rather they are the caregivers. They may be a grandparent, an auntie or uncle, or an older sibling. What distinguishes them as "perfect parents" is their unconditional loving, supportive relationship with the students and their attention to the education of their charges.

Note that perfect parents don't have to join the PTA or PTO, attend PTA/O meetings, or volunteer once a week or even once a month in the classroom. Although these are all wonderful things to do, they are nice but not necessary, extras but not essentials, frosting and not cake. We certainly encourage these activities, but we have found some other, shared characteristics that are far more important:

They have high aspirations for their child's education and they share these aspirations with their children. The single most important characteristic of the perfect parent is that they tell their sons and daughters each day that they want them to do well in

---

[1] Henderson, A.T. and K.L. Mapp, *A New Wave of Evidence: The Impact of School, Family, and Community Connections with Schools.* Austin, TX: National Center for Family and Community Connections with Schools, Southwest Educational Development Laboratory, 2002.

school and they have aspirations for them to attend and succeed in college, graduate school, and beyond. Research consistently reinforces the powerful positive impact of teachers having high expectations for every student. Less known but equally valid research illustrates how important it is for parents to have and articulate those same expectations and aspirations. In fact, the correlation between parental aspirations and student achievement is a .398.[2] For those new to statistics in the world of education, that correlation is high. Moreover, research has also shown that the students of parents who were highly engaged when they are in high school and college are more than three times as likely to graduate from college.[3]

They get their students to school on time every day. That sounds simple. But with the demands of the workplace, many parents may have to leave the house before their children. And on a good day getting a ten-year-old out the door is a challenge and just getting a sixteen-year-old upright by 7:00 a.m. is a monumental victory. Perfect parents have systems and backup systems to get their children up, dressed, and out the door to arrive at school on time.

The children are clean, fed, and ready to learn. Getting students to the bus, early morning childcare, or school is a challenge, yet the perfect parent does this and more. They assure that their children have and wear clean clothes, are washed, have brushed their teeth, and ate breakfast at home or will be at school in time to eat it there. As leaders, especially if we do not have young children at home, we forget how difficult the morning routine can be. We are too quick to blame and not quick enough to reward and encourage.

They look at their children's work each day and help them keep a calendar of exams and major assignments. The perfect parent sets aside a few minutes to go through the backpack. They

---

[2] Fan, X. and M. Chen, *Parental Involvement and Students' Academic Achievement: A meta-analysis.* Arlington, VA: National Science Foundation, National Center for Education Statistics, 1999.
[3] Eagle, E., "Socioeconomic Status, Family Structure and Parental Involvement: The Correlates of Achievement." Paper presented at the Annual Meeting of the American Educational Research Association, San Francisco, March 27-31, 1989.

look for assignments, both due and graded, and they work with the school to have the children keep a calendar of upcoming events. Most schools, beginning in the middle school grades, require some type of assignment notebook or agenda for students. Requiring students to carry these helps parents help their children.

They initiate information sharing with the school, especially at times of intense personal travails. Perfect parents do not wait for teachers to notice that something may not be quite right with a child. When the family experiences tough times, they let the teacher know through a visit, phone call, or e-mail. Most parents find it highly difficult to initiate these calls so perfect principals and perfect teachers establish and communicate processes that make this less threatening and more welcoming.

They make positive remarks about the teachers and schools at home, in the neighborhood, and on the sidelines or in the stands at sporting events. A corollary is that they do not undermine the school. Parents who did not like school as children imprint their attitudes on their own children. Parents who have had even one negative experience are also likely to share their perception with their child.

They don't miss a parental conference. Perfect parents recognize that the partnership between home and school is necessary to a child's success and never pass up the opportunity for a face-to-face with the teacher. If work prevents them from attending, they find someone who can participate, e.g. a grandparent, uncle, aunt, or even older sibling.

They take an interest in school without hovering. Perfect parents excel at communicating their interest and aspirations for their child's education by dialogue and not by questions. "What did you do in school today?" is not a conversation starter. Sharing their own school experiences, reacting to books their child is reading, or just discussing current events related to schooling and education show children that their parent is interested.

They support their children's growth into independent thinkers and young adults with a character all their own. Perfect parents appreciate the unique personality of their students and allow them to blossom rather than push them to be something the parent thinks they are or should be. The loudest parents on the sidelines are usually guilty of living through their children and not letting them develop. Also, perfect parents let their children debate and negotiate. They encourage them to have different opinions rather than to slavishly submit to the parents' will.

They get them to bed on time. Talk about easier said than done! I can't even get our three-year-old grandson to bed at 8 p.m., much less our high schooler by 10. What I can do is provide conditions conducive to their getting a good night's sleep. Reading a story to the young one, playing some music, and keeping the lights off usually works pretty well. With the oldest—perfect parents out there, please tell us what you do! With parental controls we can shut down computer access at 10 and keep the television off but, as any high schooler can tell you, there are plenty of distractions to keep the mind roiling until midnight.

Parental Engagement

A recently released report from the Appleseed's "Leave No Parent Behind" project, "It Takes a Parent: Transforming Education in the Wake of the No Child Left Behind Act" and other recent research describe in great detail the importance of parental involvement. In addition to improving student achievement, we know strong family engagement improves teacher morale and attention[4] and boosts support for district funding initiatives, such as passing a bond issue or generating donations to a district foundation. Needless to say, high parental engagement has also been shown to improve attendance, strengthen social skills, and reduce drug and alcohol use, as well as incidents of violent behavior.[5] In addition, we have read and heard about the importance of parental involvement, but we don't always know what it looks like. Too often parental involvement is misconstrued as being room parents, volunteering regularly in school, and joining the PTA/O. In fact, the Southwest Educational Development Laboratory meta-analysis of parent involvement research has synthesized four myths of parent

---

[4] Henderson, A.T. and K.L. Mapp, *op.cit.*
[5] District Management Council, "Promoting Educational Achievement through Family Engagement," DMC: Cambridge, MA, 2007.

involvement[6] and their first is: "As a parent, the best way to get involved in my child's education is by joining the local parents' organization."

Truth be told, the term "parental involvement" evokes the "fingernails-on-the-chalkboard" reaction from me. It is a demeaning term that is grounded in a "deficit model." In other words, rather than assuming that parents do not want to be engaged and preaching to them about what they need to do, we should find ways to help them do what they know is best for their children. From here on, then, I will talk about the engagement of the perfect parents and about partnerships with those perfect parents as these terms really reflect what matters most. Here are some examples of what engaged parents do to help their students and build partnerships.

- Contribute time and energy to help their children grow academically.
- Read to their children or read with them. For older students, while their son or daughter is reading an assignment or book, engaged parents read their own book. (We hear that *What Every Superintendent and Principal Needs to Know: School Leadership in the Real World* is quite a page turner!)
- Initiate the call to the school when they see something is bothering their child.
- Provide resources to support schoolwork and homework. Resources can be something as simple as a comfortable chair that the child can call his or her own.
- Encourage and assure that students complete their own work and projects.
- Be willing to sacrifice or delay their own interests and needs to their children's.
- Demonstrate that they do their homework and insist that their children do theirs.
- Initiate conversations and talk with, not at, their children.

---

[6] To see "The Four Myths of Parent Involvement in Schools" digitally, go to http://www.projectappleseed.org/4myths.html.

The Care and Feeding of Perfect Parents

As with perfect principals and professionals, perfect parents are made, not born. It is our job as educators to nurture them and help them become partners. A true partnership is also made, not born. Parents have many reasons why they are not involved with school. They may have had bad experiences themselves. In fact, Sara Lawrence Lightfoot's work, *The Essential Conversation*,[7] posits that most parent conferences are really about their own childhood experiences in relation to teachers and schools, while some parents are just apathetic or overwhelmed. *Chicago Tribune* feature writer Stephanie Banchero's series[8] profiling a well-meaning parent who took advantage of NCLB's school choice option simply could not follow through to get her eager, talented daughter to school every day. More often than not, parents are just too busy.

In addition to some parents' poor experiences at school when they were children, their sense of being overwhelmed, and their lack of time, there are other areas where barriers exist. The District Management Council[9] details three:

Administration Centered

- Failure to adopt family engagement as a central strategy for achieving educational gains
- Predominant focus on NCLB accountability provisions
- Insufficient planning
- Poor organization
- Ill-defined or undefined measures to evaluate effectiveness.

Parent Centered

- Lack of time
- Limited English proficiency

---

[7] Lightfoot, Sara Lawrence, *The Essential Conversation: What Parents and Teachers Can Learn from Each Other.* New York: Random House, 2003.
[8] Banchero, S., "One girl's struggle to find a future," *Chicago Tribune*, July 18, 2004 and "Starting over," *Chicago Tribune*, July 20, 2004.
[9] District Management Council, *op. cit.*

- Lack of efficacy in dealing with teachers and administrators (in other words, they believe that whatever they say or do is never heard or does not matter)
- Family structure (single parents, presence of a parental "boyfriend/girlfriend")
- Dual working families
- Family mobility

Teacher Centered

- Insufficient teacher time
- Lack of training in family engagement
- Negative attitudes toward parental partnership
- Concern about giving up power and decision-making authority (teachers fear that highly engaged parents will want too much say in how they run their classrooms)
- Misperceptions (usually underestimating parents' abilities)
- Safety, security and confidentiality concerns (teachers worry, arguably with justification, that parents may talk literally "out of school" about the performance and behavior of specific children in the classroom)

My wife Jan and I can identify with some of these barriers since we raised both boys while we both worked full time and then some. We have experienced more than one instance of "lack of efficacy." At parental conferences Jan had to kick me hard under the table to keep me from demanding that a teacher actually teach Michael to write and edit. In turn, I almost had to restrain her when a teacher ignored her concerns and questions and spoke for ten minutes about her own kid.

The three of us writing this book, like all teachers and leaders of a perfect school, believe that these barriers can all be overcome. Here are some ideas that worked for us, we found in research, and/or that friends and colleagues used and shared that may be helpful to parents who lead extremely busy lives.

Remind parents to parent first. Parents must know that the most important "involvement" they can have is to help their children succeed. As Project Appleseed notes, "Most important is the *parents' attitude toward learning.* Working parents may not have much time to be involved at their children's schools, but they can show how much they value education and take an active interest in what their children are learning." If they do nothing else than check the backpack every night, look over their children's homework, read to them, and spend time talking about school—both about the child's experiences and the parents' experiences at their age—they get an A+ for involvement. Although we love having parents present at school functions, parenting at home is the most important thing that perfect parents can do.

At the Board level, insist upon a written policy promoting family engagement and home school partnerships. As simple as this sounds, it is a critical first step. Parents and staff must know that home-school partnerships and parental engagement are not just empty words but are literally written policies of the District. Thus, these policies must be published and regularly communicated.

Encourage parents to communicate with teachers and train teachers to communicate with parents. Let parents know that teachers are eager to hear from them and are prompt about returning calls. The more teachers know about their children, the more they can do for them. Since finding face-to-face conference time is almost impossible for busy parents, they must know that teachers are eager to communicate by phone or e-mail whenever the school or parent has something to discuss or share. Even "e-involvement" can pay enormous dividends.

Allow them to pick and choose, divide and conquer. Faced with a plethora of activities, empathize with parents that we are all overwhelmed at times. Beginning in middle school, Jan and I decided that someone from the family would attend every orchestra and choir concert, every teacher parent and IEP conference, every sporting event, and at least one PTA meeting, one school fundraiser, and one community forum. By "family" we included Joey's brother, stepsister, grandmother, and best friend's parents. With the exception of parent and IEP conferences, it was rare that Jan and I both made the same event, but one of us or someone in the "extended" family made them all. From our son's perspective, he loved having his older brother at an orchestra concert and seeing his buddy's mom at his classroom plays or presentations as much as he loved having us there.

From our perspective, we made a contribution to the school by supporting the activities and functions, even if we could not be at every meeting or serve on long-term committees. From the school's perspective, the teachers and parents were pleased that we did what we could. What matters most to us as educators is that parents are involved in their child's education in some way. Parents should know that whether they are a "regular" at every game, PTA/O meeting, or SIP meeting or whether they just attend one special event, the school is glad that they are there for their kids and their schools.

Conduct home visits. Perfect schools find a way to get where parents are. They encourage, incite, train, and support the teachers to meet the parents in their homes, in their church basements, and in their parks.

Learn their names and something about them. In the perfect school, teachers know the parents by first and last names. They work to develop a relationship based on mutual love, respect, and admiration for their children.

Hold a "second cup of coffee." The perfect school is the perfect host. Principals and teachers find a way to sit down to "break bread" with parents. When they come to school, they treat them like guests in their home. They understand that for most parents, school was not a welcoming, nurturing, supportive environment, so the "second cup of coffee," "teas," and sharing an afternoon dessert ("pie with the principal") can create a new setting that enables parents to feel comfortable in school.

Run a book club. In some perfect schools principals and teachers conduct book clubs for students and parents. All read a book and discuss it. The books do not have to be educational books at all. A couple of our teachers had enormous success with Agatha Christie mysteries.

Host a family dinner at school. In previous research for a study on high-poverty high-performing schools, I discovered schools that actually held family dinners once or twice a month. Sitting with a family or two, teachers could model the structure of a family dinner and help parents appreciate the time with their children without distractions of television, computer games, or sirens.

Bring families on field trips. Field trips are the highlight of many students' school year, especially in impoverished communities where parents cannot afford the money or time to take kids to a museum, the zoo, or the lakefront.

Sit in on parent conferences. In truth, school leaders have far less impact on encouraging parental involvement than teachers do. It is incumbent upon leaders to reinforce this bond by setting an example. We recommend that principals sit in on parent conferences, conduct conversations, and model how to make someone feel welcome, comfortable, and be willing to talk.

Hold English classes. One of the biggest barriers to parental involvement comes from the many parents who don't speak English. Their children quickly outdistance them, and they tend not to get involved in school because of the language barrier, their home culture, and even simple embarrassment. A perfect school can use teachers to teach English to parents who do not know the language. Though the after-school and evening programs do not teach much more than basic conversation, parents light up at the chance to learn simple vocabulary, to engage with teachers, and to be part of their child's school.

Find other message carriers. An Indiana colleague of ours has had enormous success in using the churches in her community as locations to meet parents one night a week or between services. Working with the priests and ministers, she has them deliver her messages about helping their students, talking to teachers, and assuring they take care of their children's basic needs.

Train all classroom volunteers. We have visited and experienced perfect schools that actually have a curriculum and mandated three to six hours of training for classroom volunteers. They show parents how to work with kids, stress repeatedly the importance of confidentiality, and clearly distinguish their role from the teacher's and the paraprofessional's roles.

Summary

Perfect parents are not always perfect in the traditional sense, nor are they always parents *per se*. The perfect parent is an adult who cares deeply and personally about how a child is doing in school and provides the support to assure that the child succeeds. Most importantly, perfect parents put the interest of their children first and work hard to communicate with the school, get their well rested and fed charges to school on time, and talk with their children about school every day.

As leaders, we need to uncap the perfect parent potential in every adult and help them become engaged partners in their children's education and the life of our schools. Having an open-door policy is not enough. We need to go out the open door, get out of the school, and find ways to bring parents into the life of the school and sometimes into the life of their children. Understanding and overcoming the many barriers is essential. From establishing written polices at the district level to including families in classroom field trips, as well as engaging in a myriad of other activities like hand delivering parent night presentations, hosting family dinners at school, having a second cup of coffee at the community center, and hosting English classes will make a difference. The goal of the perfect school is to make parents partners. When that happens, student achievement increases, staff morale soars, parents' loyalty is strengthened, and a palpable buzz spreads throughout the community.

Knowledge rests not upon truth alone, but upon error also.

Carl Jung (1875-1961)

Chapter Four

The Perfect Principal

Max McGee

The perfect school must have the perfect principal, or at least the "practically perfect principal" because no principal can be or should be everything to everyone. The practically perfect principal (1) builds a perfect school around a shared vision, (2) is a terrific communicator, (3) is highly resourceful, (4) compiles and analyzes data to share with his or her staff, and (5) leads a balanced life which includes having fun at work.

Diogenes' search for the honest man is quite literally legendary. His quest, however, is arguably less daunting than our search for the perfect principal. In fact, the perfect principal is a paradox, for the leader who is perfect for parents is frequently far from perfect to most of the staff. Principals who are perfect for the staff by definition cannot always be perfect for all students. And a perfect principal to one teacher can easily be a lousy principal to another. Like beauty, as the following examples illustrate, perfection is very much in the eye of the beholder.

Overbearing parents believe the perfect principal is one who does their bidding, like acceding to demands to change a class placement, intervening in a minor classroom disciplinary incident, or absolving their child when he bullies another. This principal is likely to be perceived as a less than perfect "soft touch" by his teachers. Likewise, the perfect principal to one teacher may be one who is working hard to remove an incompetent colleague, yet to that colleague, his group of friends, and most likely the teachers' union, the principal is a rat. To an insecure teacher, the perfect principal backs every disciplinary decision, right or wrong. That principal, however, would undoubtedly be labeled as "unfair" or, more accurately, "wimpy and clueless" by the students in that teacher's class.

One of my favorite memories as a principal was when a rascally fifth grader was sent to me for, in the words of the teacher, "serious disciplinary action." My secretary told me that the teacher sent him to be disciplined because he had been "mouthy" with her and should have a detention. Though Jim was full of personality, I didn't picture him as one to get into a confrontation with a teacher. Arming myself with my sternest principal face, I sat him in front of my long desk. Trying to appear as tall and imposing as possible, I peered over it and gruffly asked, "What are you doing here, young man?"

"I got in trouble," he answered.

"Yes, you did. What did you do wrong?"

"Nothing really."

"Nothing? Mrs. Dour said that you were rude to her and mouthy. Just what happened?"

"I asked if I could go to the washroom, and she said in front of everyone, 'What's the magic word?' So I said, 'Abracadabra' and everyone started laughing."

I tried to keep up my game face, but then I cracked up. "That really *is* funny," I chuckled. So much for "serious disciplinary action."

And so much for being the perfect principal. Taking a student's side rarely wins points with teachers, especially ones who cannot laugh at themselves. I decided that Jim did not deserve a detention but rather an audition as a stand-up comic for our next talent show. He went back to class, and Mrs. Dour got mad at me and complained to her friends. Though most of the others in the school would have handled the matter exactly as I did, they naturally clucked and shook their heads to her face. Then they went on about their business as did I, the less-than-perfect principal.

A serious hunt for perfection among principals depends so much upon perception that it is fruitless. That said, there are some distinguishing characteristics, behaviors, knowledge, skills, and attitudes/dispositions that are possessed by better principals— which we define as those who have a sustained positive impact on teaching and learning. They aren't perfect, so for our purposes in this book let's call them "practically perfect principals." Those we can find.

What, then, are the qualities of a practically perfect principal? Are they innate or learned? What does the practically perfect principal do differently from other principals? What can we learn from practically perfect principals? Great principals have many wonderful qualities and characteristics, and other books have been written about them. Using this research, but more importantly, quite literally a century of experience, we have selected a few that distinguish the practically perfect from the simply great.

Vision

Practically perfect principals have vision and are driven by mission. Neither the vision nor mission belongs exclusively to the school or the principal. It comes from and belongs to everyone in the school. In *Fierce Conversations*, Susan Scott writes, "Few, if any, forces in human affairs are as powerful as a fierce vision."[1] The practically perfect principal is the rare individual who creates this shared vision. How does he do it? He begins by building relationships with teachers, staff, and parents. He doesn't begin by writing something about "lifelong learning" and "responsible global citizens." As relationships develop through conversations, the principal develops a profound understanding of the potential his school has, of what it can be for students, for teachers, for parents, for the community, for the district, and beyond. It takes many "fierce conversations" to uncover the essence of the school, to realize its potential, to imagine its possibility.

The shared vision, then, does not spring from the head of Aphrodite or the cerebrum of the practically perfect principal; rather, it emerges through informal conversation and formal dialogue. It is forged in discussions about the hopes and dreams for individual students, in taking new parents around the school, in visiting classes, and actively participating in formal meetings; it's done one-on-one and with small groups, departments, and staff.

---

[1] Scott, Susan. *Fierce Conversations: Achieving Success in Life and at Work One Conversation at a Time.* p. 57.

Once the practically perfect principal finds the vision, the mission statement almost writes itself, absent of jargon but dense with aspiration. Inspirational, aspirational, and perspirational, the shared vision gets people thinking, working, and believing together. Here are two exceptional examples and one that will be forgotten as soon as it is read:

- Teaching tomorrow's leaders
- To commit minds to inquiry, hearts to passion, and lives to the service of humanity
- Our mission is to provide educational experiences in a safe and secure environment that will enhance the self-esteem of all students, create a passion for lifelong learning, and develop global citizens that demonstrate responsibility and compassion for others.

What happens when there is a shared vision is that the impossible becomes achievable. The practically perfect principal's school with 75% low-income students has 80% of them meeting state standards year after year. Awards are won and recognition is achieved, i.e., in Illinois, they are the Spotlight Schools; in South Carolina, the Lighthouse Schools. More importantly, the staff becomes a real team on a "moral mission" to make a deep, lasting difference in the lives of students. As the teachers at one of these schools, Whittier School in Peoria, say, "We are responsible for student achievement. When a child fails, it is our responsibility. Children come to us with a great deal of baggage. We set that aside and teach them. If a child does not do well in our classroom, we reevaluate our teaching rather than make excuses, and *we never give up!*"[2] Teacher efficacy abounds and learning flourishes.

Getting "Out and About"

The practically perfect principal doesn't spend a lot of time in her office. She is in classrooms every day and learns the names of students and staff. More importantly, she learns who they are and

---

[2] Sara Thomas, in a speech at the Measured Progress Education Leaders Summit, Oak Brook, Illinois, October 12, 2005.

what matters to them. She appreciates their unique personalities and knows what they like to do for fun as well as their professional goals and special strengths. From being out and about, she learns how to communicate with each one and thus informs, guides, directs, cajoles, or even confronts them to help them excel.

When the practically perfect principal visits classrooms, she may pop in and out or stay for an extended time. In all cases, she is always there, in the present, with nothing more important to do. Like all great leaders, the practically perfect principal has a quality of making every individual feel like the most important person in the room when she talks to them. When she converses with someone, she talks with them (not at them), listens closely, and interacts with head and heart. Many practically perfect principals also follow up their visits with short handwritten notes complimenting teachers on what they have seen.

The practically perfect principal is also out in the community. She gets to know parents as people and makes contributions to the neighborhood. She has the courage to conduct home visits and meet individuals where they work. Residents recognize her on the street and the backyard buzzword is positive because being visible demonstrates that she truly cares and understands the importance of the school to the community. She generally joins a service or community organization, such as Optimist, Rotary, Lions, or Kiwanis, but more important than just joining, she becomes active in their work. She may chair a committee, hold an office, sit on the Board of Directors, serve as the master of ceremonies at a dinner, or make some occasional presentations about her school. She truly "walks the talk" of community partnership.

Resourceful

The practically perfect principal is resourceful. He is creative at getting what the school needs for teaching and for learning to flourish. Practically perfect principals with whom we have worked have been able to:

- Help teachers expand their classroom libraries
- Put more technology in their classrooms
- Assure that all students have a good breakfast
- Develop after-school programs and services

- Help the brightest students be challenged each day
- Arrange supplemental support for struggling students
- Assist parents in obtaining doctors and dentists for their children

Many of these took extra money and all took extra time. What the practically perfect principals did, though, was identify the problem; work with staff, parents and administrators to craft creative solutions, and stay on the issue until it was resolved. After the initial idea, then, the practically perfect principal follows through with relentless persistence. Their hard work recalls Thomas Edison's words, "Genius is one percent inspiration and ninety-nine percent perspiration."[3]

In fact, getting the job done is what drives the practically perfect principal. Although there are many sound reasons for not being able to find a solution to a difficult problem, there is *always* one that works. The practically perfect principal finds it. In the words of my mentor, Dr. Mark DeLay, "Don't tell me why it can't be done, find a way to get it done."

Let's study an example. A common complaint from a teacher or parent is that a talented child is not being challenged. The less than practically perfect principal generally responds with one or a litany of obstacles or excuses:

- State money for gifted education has been cut
- Your child did not pass the screening test for gifted services
- We cannot provide special programming because it would be a precedent for other children
- The other children will catch up
- We really don't have the resources to give the kind of support you demand
- Other parents send their children to special classes or work with them at home
- We are a public school, not a private school
- Our priority is to work with those who have special needs and are struggling

---

[3] Josephson, M., **Edison, A Biography**. New York: Francis Parkman Prize Edition History Book Club, 2003.

- The district's budget for additional materials for gifted students was reduced

The "solutions" never address the problems. Here are some particularly ineffective ones that we have heard:

- Let's have him/her tutor or teach other students in the class who don't catch on as quickly
- Why don't you go to the library and get some challenging books?
- We'll provide extra enrichment worksheets
- Perhaps our school isn't right for you and you should explore a private school
- He can spend some extra time with this computer software

As a result, the child is not challenged and both the student and parent get the message that being smart has negative consequences and excellence really doesn't matter.

Solutions that practically perfect principals develop look much different. Consider these:

- We will provide your son or daughter with some challenging problems to solve, books to read, and find a little time to work with him individually
- We will let him take his math/reading/writing, etc. class with the next grade
- Though our day is filled, we are creating a lunch bunch for a small group of students like your child to meet and discuss great books/work on intriguing problems, etc.
- We can set your middle school student up with an online high school course that will really challenge him and keep him engaged
- Your daughter will be given different assignments, not more work, and these will be individually designed to engage and challenge her, not just review what she already knows
- We have found a few others like your son or daughter and next year we will place the four of them in the same class with a teacher who realizes and can address their unlimited potential

The bottom line is that the practically perfect principal is resourceful and finds a way to get things done for his school, his staff, and for himself rather than having things done to him, his teachers, or his school.

Using Data to Move from Great to Greater

If nothing else, the practically perfect principal is all about making progress, moving from here-to-there each day and here .... to .... there each year. As noted above, she is capable of creating a shared vision and a culture of school improvement. She is also accountable and holds others accountable for getting the job done. How does she do this? She is "data driven." Does it work? Yes, if the principal has the knowledge to identify what data matters most and to analyze and communicate it to staff and parents in a manner that is clearly understandable.

The practically perfect principal looks at several data sources with colleagues to determine what needs to be done, then prioritizes the needs. The practically perfect principal who uses several data sources knows that state test scores and even norm referenced tests have a goldmine of information, especially for identifying school and district level issues, like criterion reference tests, grades, and more innovative tests such as Measures of Academic Progress (MAPs) or Scantron's Performance Series assessments. Students take these tests on a computer and depending on how they are answering the test questions, these programs adjust the difficulty of the test. If a student begins to miss several questions at the beginning of the testing session, the program makes the adjustment a bit easier and then they get progressively harder. If the student answers several in a row correctly, the programs increase the difficulty of the assessment. When the students get to the level where they cannot answer a series of more difficult questions, they have reached their instructional level. These tests are an important source of information about individual students and help teachers accurately match their teaching to each student's instructional level. Additionally, more sophisticated schools and districts have also begun using several different surveys to examine school climate, to identify problems with curriculum and instruction, and to highlight areas for improvement. (For example, in Wilmette we survey teachers every other year with the Harris Interactive Survey and a jointly designed online Union/Administration survey. We also contract with an independent organization to conduct telephone interview surveys of 300 parents and take a variety of short polls on specific issues.)

The practically perfect principal knows that all of this data can quickly overwhelm the most well-meaning staff so she carefully picks colleagues and critical friends to help sort through the findings, determine which trends are significant and which are due to chance, and which are the most important. Finally, she uses data to decide which specific priorities will have the most impact on teaching and learning. She doesn't allow herself, her school improvement team, or others to get sidetracked by opinion instead of fact or by trivial findings which need addressing.

For example, a recent school study showed that by several measures boys significantly lagged behind girls in reading and language arts. Data also showed that 53% of parents were not satisfied with the student lunches and 9% wanted some type of gifted program. Although all the findings are important, the principals were challenged to keep focused on the big item that had the most impact on learning—the gender issue—and leaving the other two for possible action in a year or two.

The practically perfect principal also has enough statistical savvy or enough friends who have such savvy to really understand when declines or discrepancies are significant or due to chance. Generally, using performance levels (like meets, exceeds, or is below state standards) does not provide the quality of quantitative information to make good instructional decisions. One really has to use the scale scores of individual students and groups and track the progress of each child from one year to the next to assure that he or she is learning and progressing.

Once data identify the gaps, the practically perfect principals must collaborate with staff to define a very small number of clear goals with specific measures and deliverables. We believe that school improvement plans should have no more than three goals or staff time and attention will get diluted, it is more difficult to achieve consensus about priorities, and the staff is set up for frustration because fully achieving four or more goals is futile. The goals need to be ones that really make a difference and that are aspirational.

Writing clear, measurable goals was thoroughly covered in a full chapter in our first book, ***What Every Superintendent and Principal Needs to Know,*** so we won't repeat it here. Instead, let's share two examples:

1. To improve transitions for students moving from grade to grade and school to school within our District.
2. To close the middle school gap in grades, state test scores, and local assessments between the boys and girls in reading and writing.

Once goals are set, the practically perfect principal and the school improvement team develop concrete measures and specific deliverables by which they will both determine progress through the year and gauge their success at the end of the year. Deliverables and measures also create opportunities for the principal to distribute leadership and accountability for achieving the goal.

Measures are nothing more than measurable results. For example, a measure for the two goals above would be:

1.1 On the independent telephone survey 90% of parents will agree or strongly agree that within the first day or two of school their children's teachers had a solid understanding of their child's academic strengths and weaknesses as well as their unique personality.

2.1 The grade point difference between seventh and eighth grade boys and girls will be reduced by 50% (from a 0.4 difference to a 0.2 difference) in two years.

Deliverables are actual products that are produced. They are not activities; those are what the staff actually does to achieve the goal, reach the measure, or produce the deliverable. Deliverables are something you can hold. Here are three examples: two are deliverables and one is an activity. Which is which?

*   All middle school teachers will attend at least one professional development session about closing the gender gap.
*   Classroom libraries will contain multiple sets of "boy's books" for independent and required reading.
*   The principal will prepare a written analysis of 30 pilot "intake conferences" held between teachers and parents just prior to the beginning of school.

The first is the activity, one used to measure 1.1 above. A classroom library often buys "boy's books," such as **The Baseball Encyclopedia, Great Battles of World War I**, and **Nothing but the Truth**. These are actual products that a teacher or group of teachers could be in charge of delivering. The written analysis is also a deliverable. (The intake conferences are both activities and actual products or deliverables.)

To move his building from good to great and great to greater, the practically perfect principal creates a real learning community by assuring that all teachers have the common knowledge and skills to understand the goals and achieve them. In fact, professional development is tied to one of the school improvement goals and specifically results in measures being achieved and/or deliverables being completed. The practically perfect principal realizes that professional development is not about a teacher pursuing further education that will make him or her a better teacher, rather it is about making a contribution to the greater good—the school or district. As Richard Elmore notes, "Professional development is effective only to the degree that it engages teachers and administrators in *large-scale improvement*... Professional development must support a *collective good* and its value judged by what it contributes to building individual capacity to improve the quality of instruction *in the school and school system.*"[4]

Communicate More Information More Often

Above all, perhaps, the practically perfect principal is an exceptional communicator. He excels at communication in many venues and in many media. He creates a core message with main message points that captures the essence of the school and the shared vision. These are repeated or inferred in nearly every communication and at every opportunity. The practically perfect principal also shares real examples of them in action. Some "main message points" we find particularly powerful are:

---

[4] Elmore, R., **Bridging the Gap Between Standards and Achievement: The Imperative for Professional Development in Education**.

- We treat your children like our own.
- There is no ceiling on your child's potential.
- Partnerships with parents are essential for children to succeed.

The practically perfect principal wakes up thinking about communication. He makes a point of meeting with key individuals face-to-face every day because through those contacts credible messengers will carry the message. By what other means does he spread the vision?

- He sends frequent notes home to parents
- He uses existing media, like the monthly PTA or school newsletter
- He seeks novel ways of reaching people like the televised local cable access forums
- He offers "second cup of coffee" meetings
- He organizes "fun (not fund) raisers" such as Daddy-Daughter Dances
- He provides a night at the ball park, spelling bees for parents, and scores of other parent-related activities

As a good communicator, the practically perfect principal is highly responsive. Phone calls and e-mails are promptly acknowledged and turned around within 48 hours. When parents, teachers, or others criticize and complain, the practically perfect principal responds respectfully but assertively, always focusing on children and the mission of the school.

Good communicators never forget that internal communication is more critical than external communication. Principals are not the only ones who do not want to be surprised. The same can be said of teachers and parents. All initiatives, goals, and important messages are shared with staff first because, in the long run, they will be heard more often and more credibly than the principal. Strong internal communication also enables the practically perfect principal to listen and learn and perhaps modify any message being released externally. Communication is truly key to the practically perfect principal's success.

The practically perfect principal has many other powerful characteristics and qualities. Beyond the basics already discussed, five others deserve quick mention.

The practically perfect principal has a balanced life. He has an incredible work ethic and puts his heart into the school, but he also makes time for his family and for himself. His family is an energizing source of renewal and he leaves his job at the office so he can give them the quality time and attention they need and deserve. He balances his work with exercise, reading, hobbies, or other pursuits that allow him to both balance all the demands of his job and to grow.

The practically perfect principal has fun. For the practically perfect principal, work itself is fun and life is good. She is optimistic and upbeat. She is serious but doesn't take herself too seriously. Laughter abounds at home and work; people feel positive in her presence.

The practically perfect principal makes a contribution beyond the district walls. He supports his colleagues and challenges them to excel. He doesn't wait for district goals and initiatives to be issued from on high but helps shape them. He works with colleagues outside the district to improve the profession and finds himself fighting for the benefit of students he doesn't know and may never see. The practically perfect principal realizes that contributing to the greater good will help make the world a better place for his students and set an example of service to an ideal and to a profession that will inspire his teachers and colleagues.

The practically perfect principal realizes that great leaders develop great leaders. She uses principles of distributed leadership to identify staff members with leadership potential and gives them opportunities to use it with parents and teachers. These future leaders have meaningful responsibilities beyond their classroom duties and really take charge of driving improvement initiatives.

The practically perfect principal is adept at hiring practically perfect teachers. In another chapter we explore what a practically perfect teacher is, but what we say will not be news to the practically perfect principal. He is capable of recognizing and developing talent, aggressive in pursing the best teachers, and reluctant to grant tenure to anyone who is mediocre.

Summary

Though the perfect principal is a mythical, elusive being, it is possible to be a practically perfect principal whose vision and daily work have long-term positive impacts on teaching and learning. The practically perfect principal creates a shared vision of high expectations and assures that all students succeed in reaching or surpassing them. Students, staff, and community know her because she seldom sits at her desk and is constantly interacting with others. An "open door policy" does not mean her door is always open, it means she opens it up and goes into the school and community. He excels at hiring good teachers and making them great as together they move their building from great to greater. The practically perfect principal understands and uses data from multiple sources to set real goals with specific measures and deliverables, and he makes himself accountable for achieving them. Reaching out to parents and contributing to the greater good, the district, the community, and the field are daily work of the practically perfect principal. Good humor, good grace, and a good deal of effusive, contagious optimism round out the practically perfect principal. He or she will make mistakes and will stumble, but the practically perfect principal quickly learns from these and moves forward a little bit wiser and healthier.

Chapter Five

Service Makes or Breaks the Perfect School

Jim Burgett

The perfect school (1) understands the difference between ordinary and quality service, (2) develops and implements a set of basic service guidelines, (3) doesn't leave service to chance, but provides extensive training for all employees, and (4) promotes an organizational ownership of service through empowerment, a common language, and a clear and meaningful mission.

Nothing can break a school system, deflate morale, or diffuse the excitement of learning as much as poor service or a general lack of character. With all the right ingredients you will be on the road of excellence to a perfect school, but even if you have the best staff, the most effective processes, and great facilities, if you lack the desire to serve, you will be average at best. This section looks at the two critical pillars of a strong educational climate: serving others and exercising strong values.

Service

In this chapter we will compare the schoolhouse to any company, business, or organization known to provide service, and then we will follow an example of one of the leading service providers in

the world. Since we know that schools can (and should) be outstanding service-providing institutions, let's also consider ten doable steps to becoming a service model that others will envy.

Big Buns Sets the Stage

Why not begin our service journey at the fictitious yet easily imag-
ined epitome of *hot cuisine,* Big Buns, a fast food restaurant chain.
Everybody knows Big Buns. You probably dined there this past
week. Drive up or walk in, it makes no difference. All you want is
to place an order, get what you request, eat it there or take it with
you, and end up gustatorily satisfied. It may not be lobster, but it
should still be a good experience. There are some pluses to the Big
Buns visit that you can count on. The bill won't break the bank.
No tipping is expected. Parking is free. The quality of the food
should adhere to an expected standard (the Big Buns triple
whammy in Houston should have exactly the same 12,450 calories
as it does in Wheeling, West Virginia). The lady or man behind
the counter will be clearly labeled as a Big Buns Host, and the ice
in your soda will be frozen. That's a lot, but not enough. The variables can make or break the experience.

Service Should Be Standard, Not a Surprise

Some things you can't be sure of when you visit Big Buns. Will
the bathroom be clean? Will the item in your bag be the same
thing you asked for? Will you be treated like a burden, an escapee,
an alien, or a customer? Will anyone at Big Buns smile? If they
forget your corkscrewed fries, will you have to argue with the
Host about who is at fault? Will they know the magic words?

Depending on the training, leadership, expectations, environment, and the personality of the "team" on hand, your experience
may vary from an F to an A+, to put it in educational terms. Too
bad; it should be an A every time. If the product is good and the

service is great, the business should be exceptional. If the product is good and the service stinks, you might give it a chance or two before driving past Big Buns and heading the extra blocks to Cholesterol Castle, with its Double Clogger. Bad service can, and will, cost business.

You know how true the example is. When you walk up to the counter at Big Buns what you really want is a smile, a pleasant greeting, a question, a repeat of the order, a cordial exchange of money, an assurance that your food is coming, and a few pleasantries along the way. When the order is handed to you, you also want another nice smile, a thank you, and—icing on the cake— maybe even a pleasant comment. The script is short and sweet and it can make all the difference in the world.

Personally, I love it when the Big Buns Host double checks my order as he/she fills the bag, when I'm thanked for my money, and when I get a smile and pleasant comment as I leave. Even "Have a nice day" is nice, if they seem to mean it. It would take only a creative second longer to say something like "Enjoy your burger and come back and see us soon."

Don't Forget to Say You Are Welcome!

Am I being sarcastic? Nope. Realistic. I'm passionate about good service. I expect it. I even help with it. When the Big Buns folk forget to thank me, I never forget to say, "You are welcome." A lonely "You are welcome" might sound a bit strange—but soon enough it might not be so lonely. When they are unpleasant, I try to be compassionate. But if they frown, say nothing positive, and forget to ask about my order, I usually ask, "Are you having a bad day? Is the Big Buns stock down? Have you forgotten your lines?" Unfortunately, it doesn't always register, but sometimes the Host does get the idea.

Good Service is Not Hard to Provide

Recently four of us were at a fancier place to eat. Not a Big Buns—a place with a menu, a waiter, and a nice black leather folder for the check. The waiter came over to us, two adult couples, and said, "Hi, kids! On vacation?" We *were* on vacation and between the four of us we have a plethora of kids and grandkids. The waiter was clean cut, well groomed, and smiling; he made us feel very comfortable. He never called us "you guys," he got the order right, and he even said things like "Good choice," "That's one of our best items," "Do you like hot spice? That one is kind of hot," and "I'll be back in a flash with your salad, but you take as long as you want eating it." He made it fun, not routine. He knew when to talk and when to listen. He was confirming, pleasant, and positive. When it came time for the black leather folder, he had earned a nice tip. The service was great. We will eat there again.

The Top Ten of Service

David Letterman started the reverse top ten craze so let me thank him for the format that follows. Alas, this top ten isn't really ranked in any particular order nor did I create or invent any of them. All ten are stolen, though from whom I have no idea. (Over the years I have attended so many workshops and read so many books about service that the sources of these ideas are long gone. How's that for a disclaimer?)

A last point: I'm passionate about providing good service. If I get carried away, I apologize.

Here we go. If you want to travel down the road of excellence toward that apex called perfection, you better equip yourselves with the skill of a service leader and provider, and be a living example of *quality* service.

Ten: There is no such thing as Selective Service.

OK, there is a Selective Service operated by the United State Government. But there shouldn't be "selective service" when it comes to being a service provider. I learned this quickly when I visited the Ritz-Carlton, the most highly acclaimed and awarded service-provider for hospitality in the world. I had a chance to go through third-party training at a Ritz-Carlton facility for several days, studying their model of service, the same model that won them the famed Malcolm Baldridge Award.

One of the most striking things I witnessed was the lack of "selective" service. What I mean by this is that they didn't provide a different level of service for different people. Granted, you are among the more financially blessed if you stay at a Ritz. They are anything but inexpensive. But the same level of service was given to visitors, people just looking around, those who came just for a drink or a meal, guests, parkers in the Ritz lots, and, most impressive of all, employees by other employees.

Over several days I saw it time and again. They exercised the same "basics," spoke the same language, and treated each other the same as they treated the paying gentry. In fact, most of the employees are just "regular Joes" and probably couldn't afford a night at the Ritz any more than most of us can, but when at work, they were treated the same as the most influential guest. That impressed me as much as anything I witnessed. It was real. It was part of their culture. It's why the Ritz-Carlton is the best in the world.

So, if a school wants to travel on the road to perfection, they have to learn the secrets of providing non-selective service. The same high service to all parties, all employees, all students, all visitors, and to each other. After all, schools are service organizations, and learning to serve without false pretense is the best way to serve anyone, anywhere, anytime.

Oh yes, one more thing. Schools are not like the Ritz or Big Buns. Most (but not all) of the people who come to the school have no other choice. Most can't afford an alternative private school and in most communities you have one school that you are assigned to and that is where you go. So, in a certain way, the audience is captured and contained. Even if you mess up, they seldom leave. Which means you have to work twice as hard in a school to provide quality service since lousy service alone won't cost you customers.

Nine: Service is Governed by the Mission.

How can a school system, or school building, operate without a mission? Even if it is a short, concise, simple statement, if it is owned by the members of the organization, the mission should be the central focus of everything you do. Everything the Ritz-Carlton does to train and promote quality service is a direct reflection of their stated mission. The parallel is obvious.

Let's say that the Ernie Banks Elementary School District has the following mission statement: "Our mission is to provide the best learning opportunities for our students, to seek and secure the best resources possible, and always to promote an attitude of caring and community." The mission must direct the level of service provided. When developing a service motto and simple "basics," they must be synchronized with the mission. For example, the "best learning opportunities" can be defined as an environment that is conducive to learning, to understanding learning styles, and to establishing an atmosphere of caring and compassion. How do you get there? Simply by serving one another in the best possible way. Service is directly related to the Mission. A service-oriented organization that uses its bonding mission as the center of all activities is headed straight toward excellence.

Eight: Create a Service Motto.

One of my favorite mottos is from the same Ritz-Carlton. "We are Ladies and Gentlemen serving Ladies and Gentlemen." They follow the motto with this statement, "As service professionals, we treat our guests and each other with respect and dignity."

In the workshops and administrative academies I offer I frequently refer to the Ritz and its service program. Often I'm asked why I compare a school district to the classiest and one of the most expensive hotel chains in the world. My response is simple: I want my school district to be considered the best of the best. Maybe not in terms of dollars spent per student or by the number of swimming pools or handball courts or the quantity of Advanced Placement courses offered, but certainly in the way we prepare students, provide an outstanding learning opportunity, are an integral part of the community, and how we respect our staff of educators. We can be the Ritz-Carlton (RC) of schools by the way we treat each other and, as their motto says, by the way we treat our guests (students, taxpayers, families) with respect and dignity. That is the essence of service.

In the programs I mentioned I also take the liberty of slightly modifying the RC motto and the 20 "basics" into language appropriate for schools. For example, I change the RC motto to read, "We are Ladies and Gentlemen serving Ladies and Gentlemen of all ages." That covers preschoolers to senior citizens.

There are several other components of the RC motto that I really like. First of all, they put the employees first by setting expectations as high for them as for the guests. "We are Ladies and Gentlemen..." Then they emphasize the focus with the word "serving." Finally, they classify their guests as "ladies and gentlemen." What a statement! It sets the standard for everyone in the system, and focuses on the number one activity, providing service. The follow-up statement is also well crafted: "As service professionals..."—not as blue collar workers, cooks, housekeepers, lawn mowers, or bellmen, but as "service professionals." In other words, in whatever we do we are indeed professionals, the best, the top of the ladder. And then it says, "...we treat our guests AND EACH OTHER with respect and dignity." There is no selective service at the RC! Everyone gets treated the right way and the same way. Everybody.

When I converted the RC Motto to a template for schools, I made only a few adjustments to the second sentence. "As educational professionals, we must treat all our students, guests, citizens, and each other with respect and dignity." A little tweaking to make it more comprehensive and inclusive for school folks.

Each district needs a motto to hang its service hat on. Not a cute little saying to memorize, but a motto to live by. At the RC every employee carries a card at all times that lists all the fundamentals, starting with the Credo and Motto. They talk about it. They live it. They expect others to honor it. If you want to raise the level of service and respect at your school, you have to take the service component seriously. It has to be there 24/7. It can't be a fad, a short-time professional development gimmick, or just another "new thing" to do. It has to be a way of life. Mottos may seem lame and useless, but if one is a benchmark for real action and behavior it can make a huge difference in developing morale, setting expectations, and building a strong foundation.

Seven: Write a Set of Basics.

The participants in my workshops about building a service model spend a great deal of time reviewing and discussing service basics. I also co-present a business model with the administrator of a hospital and he too focuses on the basics of service in his presentation. What are the basics? They are a simple list of *how* you provide service.

Let me continue to use this exemplary Ritz-Carlton model.[1]

There are 20 "Ritz-Carlton Basics." They and related items are boxed and printed so they neatly fit on a small folded card that fits into any pocket, purse, or wallet. This is the card I mentioned earlier that employees carry with them. Theirs isn't a one-time training program. It is a way of life. And it works.

I have worked with many schools who have taken the RC 20 and used it to build their own set of basics. The basics are nothing more than simple instructions or thoughts on service. They include

---

[1] The model shared here is the one in use when the author experienced his training opportunities. The Ritz-Carlton, twice given the Malcom Baldridge Award, constantly improves its service process. The Ritz-Carlton eagerly shares its efforts toward perfection; for a plethora of useful information, check its website at www.ritzcarlton.com.

the following: The Credo (or mission), the Motto, a statement of three steps of service (provide a warm greeting, anticipate needs, give a fond farewell), an "employee promise" that talks about the importance of employees and a good way of life for them, a statement on the expectation of annual training by all employees, and a commitment that all employees will know the company's objectives. The RC Basics also include a statement on employee rights, that every employee is charged with the task of continuously identifying defects throughout the organization, expectations of teamwork, how employees are empowered to solve problems, the responsibility of everyone to maintain "uncompromising levels of cleanliness," and more. Language, telephone etiquette, safety, speaking positively, escorting guests, and protecting the assets are also in the Basic 20. As important as the content is how these are written—how positive, inspiring, and confirming the statements are.

Your "basics" need to represent your organization, in no small part because they are written and "owned" by them. They must be realistic, supported, and true. They must also be reinforced—we will get to that soon. The "basics" become the cornerstone of how you provide outstanding service, service that moves you along the road of excellence toward perfection.

Six: Develop a Language

I think my favorite RC basic is number 14. It reads as follows:

> *"Smile—we are on stage. Always maintain positive eye contact. Use the proper vocabulary with our guests and each other. (Use words such as "Good Morning," "Certainly," "I'll be happy to," and "My pleasure." Do not use words such as "O.K.," "Sure," "Hi/Hello," "folks," and "No problem.")"*

You see why it's my favorite. It alone, if adopted and owned, can change the climate of any school. Imagine if the Big Buns Hosts followed this one simple guideline! They would smile, look you in the eye, and talk to you on a different and more inspiring level. Imagine asking a Big Buns Host for a packet of ketchup and getting the reply, "Certainly, my pleasure." And then, as it was handed to you, the person looked you in the eyes, smiled, and said, "May I get you anything else?" That's a far cry from a distracted look aimed somewhere in your direction and a hand poking out at you with a fist full of packets, without comment!

How about the proper language basics when you talk to students, greet the lunch lady, call a parent, drop off a form at someone's desk, address a Board member, converse with the Pepsi vendor (delivering only fruit juice or water these days), or *anyone, anywhere, all the time!* You, single handedly, can change the atmosphere and working conditions for those you meet and greet. Imagine if everybody did the same thing! Fortunately, this basic is contagious!

Five: Train, Train, Train.

To some people, providing service comes naturally. They know how they want to be treated and they treat others the same way. Some are trained through their church upbringing since serving others is the mantra of many religions. Others just use common sense, have a good feel for marketing, or are naturally more inclined to do what seems best. However, there are some folks who don't have a clue. Either they don't care about a positive, productive environment or they have had little experience with win-win situations. So they must be trained. Whatever the level of service attitude an employee has, everyone ultimately needs to be on the same page, so training for all is essential.

Workshops on how to provide and understand quality service should be mandatory for all employees and educators. Just as important is the ownership of the concept and process. Shared development of the basics, the motto, the mission, and all related information is crucial. People have a natural tendency to support something they helped develop. Providing professional service to everyone, everywhere, all the time, should be a major goal of any organization that wants to be considered excellent. Strong and positive relationships are the key to success in most institutions.

The Ritz Carlton has a wonderful model for providing training and keeping it current and alive. Not only does every employee have a copy of the basics, the motto, and the credo with them at all times, every day all employees meet for a short session to review a number of RC issues and to discuss one of the basics. The corporation provides an agenda for the meeting that has some common elements for all employees no matter where they are located. One part of the agenda includes the "basic" that will be reviewed that day. Thus, in a one-month period of time (of about 20 working days), each basic is reviewed. This is in addition to annual and specialized training. The RC takes professional development very seriously and uses every opportunity to learn from their employees as well as train them. The sessions allow two-way dialogue that reinforces what works and constantly improves processes, procedures, and regulations. Employees know and feel that the RC listens to them.

Why couldn't we incorporate the same concepts at our schools? Why couldn't we constantly review and update how we communicate with each other, how we handle problems, how we control conflict, and how we anticipate situations? Wouldn't a regular and frequent discussion and review of the basic components be productive? Wouldn't it be great if we talked about the Mission and what it means? Or discussed situations where service was exceptional and/or lacking? We need to talk about the basics that have been developed and share opportunities to provide better service throughout the system. Everyday meetings might not work for all situations, but for some employee groups it indeed might be appropriate. Train people how to serve others, reinforce that training on a consistent basis, and then offer new training to keep things fresh and meaningful.

Four: Evaluate.

The way to measure improvement or disaster is to evaluate. Some people fear evaluation of anything because of the potential consequences, and maybe rightly so. Thus, effective evaluation has to be non-threatening for the employee who is trying and working hard, though it *should* be threatening for the employee who does little, cares less, and does nothing to help or support the organization that he or she works for. People should feel that evaluations are there to help the good employee and thus they should actually desire them. The employee that looks at evaluation as a means of growth, higher achievement, and greater success will also work hard to do well when evaluated.

For these reasons it is imperative that schools establish a variety of means to evaluate the effectiveness of quality service. A single survey, or one small sampling of a procedure, wouldn't be enough. It will take a variety of evaluations to measure the whole picture.

These run the range from self-evaluations to polling the consumer. Instruments needn't be long, involved, or expensive. In fact, simple questions or checklists often work better than long and complicated forms. Having every third person who visits a school office write their name and address on an index card for two consecutive days, and then sending them a short survey on how they were served, if their questions were answered, etc., is a great way to "spot-check" the effectiveness of the school's service program.

Asking students, certified and non-certified staff members, that infamous Pepsi vendor, visiting parents, and maybe a handful of one-time guests how they rate the friendliness, helpfulness, and service they received is a great evaluation process.

If you want your service climate to improve, keep evaluating how it is perceived.

Three: Empower.

A concept that separates one school from another is the empowerment of the employees. I like to call it "ownership of issues." It is a simple concept in theory, but more difficult in practice. It takes a special type of administrator and system to successfully put it in place. It also crosses the lines between providing service and discipline and providing direction and problem solving.

Nothing is more frustrating than having the buck passed from one person to another. When I buy a car, I hate it when the salesperson can't answer my questions without going to the "supervisor." If my question was bizarre or totally new, I could understand the need for help. But if I'm asking for a certain price or if five oil changes come with the car, I expect the professional I am working with to help me directly. If my steak looks more like a piece of barbecued chicken than a medium rare hunk of beef I expect the waiter/waitress to be able to handle the problem without calling in the food militia. If I need directions in a school and the first person I see is the custodian or the gym teacher, I would want them to direct or take me to the place I want to visit rather than send me off in some vague direction. The short walk will also give them an opportunity to welcome me and see if I need other help, or, better, to direct me to the office to sign in.

Empowering employees to help solve problems, short-circuit simple steps, give quick information, or handle an issue directly can be immensely helpful. Don't misinterpret what I mean. I don't mean to skip the rules or make exceptions. I mean that if a student comes to a teacher with a problem that can only be answered by Mr. Jones, that teacher should have the authority to contact Mr. Jones, or take the student to see Mr. Jones, and to act as a conduit for problem solving. Rather than saying, "You need to see someone in the main office," by directly helping the student you show that you care—an attitude you will certainly help spread by your modeling.

Quality service training can provide an opportunity for a discussion on how staff members can be empowered and how they can provide outstanding assistance. You'll be amazed at how many ways you can empower educators to provide quality service.

Two: Foster Ownership.

Two of my favorite words when it comes to providing a top-notch education for students in a superior school setting are "ownership" and "passion." How far can you travel down the road of excellence toward perfection without successfully developing these two concepts?

Passion is something that identifies the best of the best. It is easy to see that passionate people love what they do. They are working in the school system because of a passion to make a difference. They don't have a job, they have a career. They take pride in their product, whether it's a clean hallway or a high-testing student, a great lunch casserole, or a child with special needs who has just learned how to sip water from a cup. They love who they work with and want them to feel the same pride that they do. They support the system and work hard for better resources and fairer funding. They understand that a school system is part of government, supported by taxes, and "owned" by the community. In other words, they get the big picture and are passionate about their part in making in work

Ownership, when adopted by a system, can literally change everything. When the school becomes owned by everyone, a sense of pride develops that is hard to measure. Ownership is related to service. Good service makes you and others feel welcome, appreciated, and special. When an auto dealer provides outstanding service, you brag about the dealership and it becomes in a strange way "your" dealership. The same is true with almost any business that has direct service contact with their customers. Why can't that be the same for a school? In some ways it is easier to feel ownership if you have long-term ties with students and families, if staff have served a long tenure, and when students' children and grandchildren attend. It becomes a place of history, of value, of the heart. Good service also makes the new resident or new teacher or new cook feel the same way by making them feel good about who they are and what they do. Simple basics, a good and livable motto, and an environment of caring provide a strong foundation for attaining the goals of success. All come from providing quality service.

Numero Uno: Never Fake the Fantastic Four.

Finally, since we are talking about service, let's peel off everything we have said so far and go back to just four fundamentals of good service: Be helpful, say please, follow up with thank you, and truly care for one another. In a nutshell, those are the basics of not only good service but also successful relationships. Can you build the "perfect" school on things you learned in preschool? Probably not, but you can certainly become a place of excellence if you embrace those four simple qualities of kindness and compassion.

It all boils down to this...

I knew of two assistant principals in the same building. One told the supporting staff members what to do. The other asked them. One expected things done on a deadline and rarely voiced any appreciation. The other established mutually acceptable timelines and always said thank you for everything his staff did. One seldom did a thing to reciprocate any help and rarely expressed any concern for the welfare of his staff. The other would do anything for anyone and always made a point of saying hello, good-bye, and knowing about families and situations. Both worked in a very successful school system under good leadership. Both were good administrators. But the environment around the thoughtful administrator was exceptional. People wanted to work for and with him. People respected and admired him. The staff looked up to him. He was a true leader, a person of excellence.

The other man was respected for his position, but not for who he was. If he left his job there would be the mandatory party with little passion. He did his job well, but he lacked simple human kindness. He promoted no ownership. He served some folks well (the higher ups, parents, and some teachers). He served others poorly and thus the environment around him was cold, even though it was moderately productive. If he was a Big Buns Host you would get your meal, the right change, and a scripted thank you—nothing more, nothing less. He would keep Big Buns profitable, but he would not promote growth. That's the bottom line. Do we want a school that just does the job or do we want an institution that does the job with quality and pride, and leaves you with a sense of wonder—like maybe you too own the place? The choice is simple and the solution is doable. Provide quality service. Always.

Chapter Six

Infuse Character, Build Characters

Jim Burgett

The perfect school (1) recognizes the importance of employing only quality people of high character; (2) develops a process for screening, interviewing, and hiring people who understand and complement the goal of excellence; (3) develops and implements a character education program for everyone (students, staff, community) that reflects the goals of excellence; (4) creates an atmosphere of ownership and pride that continually exemplifies the adopted standards of character, and (5) passionately evaluates, modifies, and continually improves the strong foundation of values and character.

Not a program but a way of life

This chapter will address character as a way of life, not as a program. We will talk about people as the key to success and about the need for visionaries, not missionaries. This chapter will help you take a school system to a new level in terms of expectations and results. We will also discuss how any school can become more than just part of the national character movement—it can have character of its own. We will also talk about finding and building *characters* that make a difference.

Where do you start taking the first step? How do you establish an attitude of excellence or perfection? There is no easy answer, but I firmly believe that a foundation of strong values, clear direction, and a universal appreciation of what is right and just must be in place before other, major changes will take place. You start there—and thus this chapter on character and characters.

We need people of character to build a school headed toward perfection. People with the courage to stand up for what is right. The gumption to question and encourage legislators. The strength to make tough decisions. The ingenuity to take meager resources and with them create productive students. And the moral integrity to do it all correctly and with vigor.

Character vs. character education

Note that I'm not discussing "character education." While character education programs can be a fundamental foundation for building and maintaining character, that isn't all of the equation. A character education program is quantitative. Character is subjective. A district or school can develop a formal and extensive curriculum based on a quality, proven character education program and teach every student about it, but that alone doesn't guarantee that the school will have character. Character is defined as a distinctive quality, as moral excellence.[1]

Four Not-So-Easy Pieces

Let me reduce the process to four steps.

- **Step One**: Develop a staff with character.
- **Step Two**: Transfer character from people to the system.

---

[1] Chapter 8 of this book talks about building an excellent work force. It discusses the often neglected art of elimination, or removal, of personnel who have not, or possibly cannot, achieve excellence in what they do. Dumping the characters and replacing them with new staff of character. Is this a swift process? Hardly. It may take years to filter out the nonproductive, ineffective, burned out, pooped out deadwood that dams the stream to perfection. Yet when you read Chapter 8, you will see that it can be done, and often should be.

- **Step Three**: Live, breathe, and exemplify the climate you have established.
- **Step Four**: Continually develop people of excellence at every station of the system.

Four not so simple, yet not so complicated, steps that pave the path to excellence.

The First Step

Develop a staff with character

Let's roll up our sleeves and get to work.

You want a perfect school? Or at least one that is heads and shoulders above the norm? You want great test scores, community support, a super staff, and a state-of-the-art everything? You begin with outstanding educators.

To understand the process you must understand my definition of educator: it is anyone involved with the process of educating. That includes the full spectrum from Board member to bus driver and everyone in between.

What values do you want your educators to demonstrate?

If systematic improvement begins with agreed-upon values, you must begin by defining your values. What values do you want in the people who educate your kids?

The road to perfection can begin with a simple discussion around a table. It may be a Board table, a lunch table, or a meeting table. It may involve a large group of leaders or just a few. But you must be there. Who are you? The leader of the pack. The visionary. The one with the guts and courage. The person who commands the charge. (That's not you? Then find that person and read this book together. He or she will need a team; you should be on it!)

Ask the right questions

Here is a sample of the questions to ask:

- What do we want our educators to be able to do?
- What qualifications can we realistically expect our staff to bring to the table?
- How will we recognize and compensate excellence?
- How can we inspire our current staff of educators to raise the bar?
- How do we replace or retire the ones that don't know how to spell the word "change"?

"Ask and the door shall be opened," I've heard said. If you ask the right questions, you usually start the right discussions that most of the time points you in the right direction. Follow up, and something gets done.

It might go like this. The leader says that the district has the ability to do better, reach a new level of excellence, jump on the road to perfection. To get there we need to start somewhere, so let's seriously talk about our weak areas. Maybe math scores are low in the middle grades. Morale stinks in the transportation department. Data shows an attendance problem at Oak Elementary. The high school principal has offered no new initiatives since the year Mama Cass died. Or Mozart. Three of the Board members take delight in voting against the other four, no matter what the question. The list goes on.

You want to develop a staff of character. A staff with values. A staff of excellence. It will be hard to move to step two if you don't get the buy-in from your educators. You need a plan. If your district is a mess, your plan will take time and exceptional persistence. If your district is humming along nicely, doing a good job, and your staff is there for the right reasons and to do the right things, the next step might be quick and easy.

Narrow the focus to a meaningful few

You decide to identify three primary needs that will help you develop a staff of character. Let's say they are to revamp the transportation department, bring some inspiration to the high school leadership, and eliminate one Board member. All are doable.

A visionary would say that you need a long-range plan. Call it *"Building the Road to Excellence."* And then you need a session to develop ownership; call it a kind of Strategic Planning. You also need a group of leaders who are on the same page. Call it the *Road to Excellence Planning Team.*

Now set the stage and do the work. Bring 10-20 of your top educators together (a comfortable blend of teachers, Board members, administrators, support staff, and others) and have a session to outline the basic beliefs you share. Maybe you review, revise, or write a Mission Statement in the process. If you want to go the next step and do a full blown Strategic Plan, go for it. The most important thing that you do here, though, is list, discuss, and own what you believe are the values you share. If you all agree that in order to provide the best educational opportunities for kids you need the best educators possible, then write it down and live by it. Use this belief to formulate a process to advertise, screen, interview, and hire employees. Use this belief when you seek replacements for Board members at the next election. Use it when you seek bids on who will provide bus or food service. If one of your basic values is that you must love working with students to participate at your district, then incorporate that expectation in all your hiring and contracting processes and philosophies.

If you agree that ethical, professional, and moral behavior should be the bedrock, then settle for nothing less. Don't just list it, live it. It might mean that you reject every candidate for a certain position because they don't fully meet your stated values and objectives. It might mean that you use substitutes for a year rather than hire a "C" teacher (especially when you have established the agreement that your teachers need to be "B" grade or better.)

Seat covers can be a start!

For example, you might take your expectations to the transportation department and compare what you want with what you have.

A true story provides a useful illustration. A new superintendent was appalled to see that many of the seats on the district's buses had been damaged. Some had pen holes poked in them. Some had words written on them. Others had tears and even long slits. Only one regular bus route in the entire fleet had a vehicle with "clean" seats (without graffiti or damage), and it was one of the oldest buses in use.

The superintendent met with all of the drivers and the transportation director. He asked why the buses looked the way they did. "Kids will be kids," "You can't watch everything," "They aren't as bad as they used to be," "We can't drive and keep the seats looking like new at the same time" were among the long list of lame excuses. Not one driver or official took ownership.

The driver who had the bus with no damage to any seat was quiet during the discussion, so the superintendent asked what she did differently. "Simple," she responded. "I have a seating chart. I check the seats after every route. If there is a problem with any seat, I tell the student assigned to that seat to clean it or we must buy a new seat. I call his/her parents if the seat needs to be replaced. I don't go through the district because the district doesn't really care. I do it." She continued, "I also check the seats before and after my bus is used for some other activity and I don't drive it. I make the other driver accountable if something happens. They know it and expect it. Only once have I had to replace a seat cover because I didn't know who cut it."

The superintendent wrote the following things on the chalkboard:

- "Expectation of the Driver"
- "Responsibility of the Student"
- "Known and Enforced Discipline"
- "Ownership by All Parties"

The superintendent then announced that during the summer all damaged seat covers on any bus would be replaced and that he would expect each driver to maintain them like new. He would support and help enforce a plan of replacement if students damaged the seats. He would expect the drivers to demand and expect compliance. A clean and well maintained bus would help with discipline and attitude. It could be done, he would do his part, and together they could make the buses cleaner and in line with the district goals. By saying this he was establishing the new "goals of the district" that all drivers would be expected to uphold.

One of the more aggressive drivers asked what many had probably been thinking, "What do you mean the 'goals of the district?'"

The superintendent was thrilled to be able to answer that question. "We want to be a district that is heads and shoulders above the norm. We want our students to be honest, ethical, hard working citizens. We want a climate based on mutual respect that includes respect for property and possessions. One of our goals is that this school system will be a good place to learn, to work, and to grow pride." He explained that in order to accomplish such lofty goals one must attend to details. The expected behavior of students on buses and the expected respect of property should be two fundamental goals that we work very hard to achieve. He asked if there were any other questions. The group silently nodded "no."

Guess what? It worked. At the end of the next full school year there were no seat covers that needed replacement, although during the year two had been replaced, each fully paid for by a student's parents. The students learned the new expectations quickly, drivers were proud of the way their buses looked and wanted to keep them looking new, and during the first year one driver asked the district for regular interior and exterior washing of the buses, something never before requested. At the end of that year the superintendent hosted a pancake breakfast for all the drivers and recognized them for the progress they had made.

Recognize the problem. Talk about it. Develop ownership in the solution. Work as a team. Reward positive change. Poof! You are on the road to developing a staff with character.

The Second Step

Transfer character from people to the system

In 1998 I attended a small group session at the annual conference of superintendents, business managers, and School Board members in Illinois. This is the "Triple I Conference" that is held in Chicago each November. I attended this small group session with one of my Board members, Mr. Rooney Barker. The session was on Character Education. A large suburban district near Chicago was sharing an exceptional program it had crafted. It involved some of the traditional character education components like key words of the month, student skits showing the words in action, and inclusion of a curriculum that taught students how to understand and incorporate such values as honesty, responsibility, caring, fairness, and citizenship. The presenters talked about how some of the schools had adopted the program and how it had spread to the community. How that the word of the month was displayed on city police cars and was seen on message boards throughout the district. They gave an inspiring and motivational presentation that showed and shared their pride in the program. They had taken key components of the best implementations they knew and had carefully crafted them into a unique program that specifically fit their district and community. Rooney and I left the meeting with pages of notes, their well-prepared handouts, and a shared thought—we can do that, and we can do it better.

Alas, the sad truth is that one Board member and one superintendent alone cannot implement such a program. But they *can* plant seeds. And plant seeds we did.

Seeds grow into VIP

We shared the session with the Board, and then I shared it with the principals. The Board gave us the go-ahead to lay the foundation for the program. No money, but lots of enthused encouragement! We met with a few key people (educators with character) and they shared some great ideas. We went to our Business Education Alliance (BEA) and asked for their support of a new program that might need some "seed" money. They gave us a small stipend. Then the hard part took place. Rooney and I backed away and gave the small group that was excited about development of this concept its own creative space. It had to become "their" project, not ours.

They ran with it! The district couldn't afford to give us any funding, but the community leaders stepped up. The BEA paid the fees for 18 staff members to attend the St. Louis Character Education Conference in the fall of 1999. By the start of school in 2000, the VIP Program was launched, based on four visionary principles. (1) Develop a district-wide program for our needs, (2) Make this an umbrella over several existing programs that were fragmented and did not articulate through many grade levels, (3) Seek community input and involvement, and (4) Establish a core committee to develop the program.

The project grew in several directions at the same time. Asked to meet and discuss the new ideas were leaders from the local parochial school, the mayors of our communities, leaders of many civic organizations, clergy from all churches, and key figures from many business organizations. The BEA became our "sponsor" but the district also contributed as best it could. "Words of the Month" became a foundation for the name Very Important Principles. A logo was established. Soon there was an Executive Committee that met monthly with representatives from every building. A VIP Coordinator was "employed" (with a tiny stipend) and students, staff, community, and representatives from literally every facet of the community started to buy in.

In our community today you will find very professional and attractive signs located in parks, along highways, and in other very visible areas that list the Very Important Principles. The first week of the month you will see the Principle for that month on billboards, displayed at City Councils, on church bulletins, flashing on signs at banks, and even on slips of paper handed out with payroll checks at some of the industries. VIP floats, handouts, and magnetic signs on buses and police cars all proudly share the "Principles." But most of all, from pre-K through high school, kids talk the VIP language and it is not uncommon for someone to comment about respect, service, fairness, self-control, citizenship, courage, responsibility, honesty, or caring. The VIP logo, a butterfly, became the project of the high school metals class and metal artwork standing 6-feet tall was crafted for each school—several are at the high school itself. Some community members and businesses even purchased some of the logos.

VIP—just another Character Education Program?

We don't call it Character Education, rather a way of life. It is proudly owned and perpetuated by our schools and community. Business leaders as well as educators talk about the values. Ministers preach them. Mayors open meetings with them. Police proudly display them. Bus drivers refer to them when working with kids. Teachers teach lessons about the Principles. The kids don't tire of the program; they are actually proud of it. It has become an important part of our community culture. It defines our environment. It is who we are. It is one more component of excellence. And if you think high school students and adults won't get involved, think again.

Don't reinvent the wheel!

Do you have to start from scratch to transfer character from staff to systems?

Not at all. Character education can be copied, learned, adapted, created, or invented. Some aspects appear in almost all programs. Want to see a variety of examples? Go to my favorite place, www.google.com, and start hunting. Character Counts is an excellent national program and has a super website. If you type in "VIP Character Education" you will see the program I just described. You can start from there. Several states have outstanding programs already available. Why reinvent the wheel?

Some basics to remember

Here are some important things to remember about developing a system-wide program of character: you must define the goals, develop a wide base of ownership, support and promote the program, and work diligently. It does take patience. It also takes people of character to develop programs based on character.

Don't let a step backward stop any forward movement. Look at the total picture now and in the future, then go for it. Remember, character is something you build over a long time through high expectations, relentless effort, and a passion for excellence.

The Third Step

Once you have it, live it.

The third step is critical: live and breathe the character climate. In the previous step we planted seeds, did the hands-on stuff of developing a program, and set some lofty expectations. Now we must put it in action. This is your part. This is where you must excel. This is leadership by example. This has nothing to do with those you hire, what programs you inspire, or how well you have "sold" character. This has to do with you. This book was written for school administrators because they play a key role in everything. A good administrator is a good manager, a good leader, and a good educator. But an excellent administrator is all of those as well as a good person, a compassionate and caring human being, and someone to be admired.

Don't be good, be exceptional

I shutter when I hear someone say, "Oh she's a good administrator, but she's kind of bossy (or dictatorial, or gossipy, or negative, or antiunion, or a bit lazy, or not very bright, or a little conceited, or unfriendly, or has favorites, or...)" You get it. I want to hear, "She's a good administrator *and* she is very caring (loves the kids, is admired by the teachers, is extremely fair, has an outstanding work ethic, would do anything for the school, is a blessing, has a great outlook, has made a difference, or...)" That's living and breathing the climate of character.

Administrators who make a difference learn early the two cardinal rules of effective leadership: never lie and never gossip. They know that in order for people to follow them, they must lead with integrity. They know that they can't just talk ethics, they must also demonstrate them. They know that hard work and caring will do more than anything else to get people to follow and understand.

"Two sets of three"

John Wooden, in his book *My Personal Best*, credits his success to the "two sets of three" that his Dad taught him and his brothers. What a difference these six little statements can make to develop outstanding administrators. "Never lie. Never cheat. Never steal. Don't whine. Don't complain. Don't make excuses."

The average administrator sends a staff member a card or gift when someone close to that person dies. The exceptional administrator does the same, but writes in their calendar on the anniversary of the death a reminder of the event, and then (on the first anniversary of the loss) sends that staff member just a short note that says "thinking about you today." Or maybe a single flower. That note or flower means more than anyone would ever imagine. That administrator lives and breathes the qualities of character. Goes the extra step. Sets the stage for a district of excellence.

The exceptional administrator sees work that doesn't meet expectations and he addresses it immediately. The exceptional administrator notes and responds to problems and situations before they get out of hand. The exceptional administrator puts others first, but never loses sight of the needs of his or her own family. That's living and breathing the values of character.

The best compliment I could ever imagine for any leader is to have others ask themselves, "What would he or she do in this situation?" When people respect your actions, they respect your leadership.

Passionately do what is right

Step three is easy to grasp but it takes focus and desire to make happen. To be the best, you have to do your best. You have to say "I'm sorry" when you screw up. You have to recognize, thank, and appreciate those who work hard, and even those who don't work hard enough but are trying. You have to say "hi" to those who might forget to say it to you, and you have to be strong enough to correct, encourage, and even dismiss those who aren't doing what's best for kids. You will never be universally liked, but you can try to be universally respected.

The Fourth Step

Develop people of character—always and in all ways

The final step, to continue to develop people of character at every station of the system. For a perfect school you need the best employees. To get the best employees you must work on every aspect of employment, retention, and development. Did you ever notice that excellent school systems usually have a very stable, satisfied, enthusiastic staff? That's not by accident. Somewhere in the system someone has taken care of the details of employment. They make sure that the district hires people of character who are highly skilled and passionate about what they do. They also have someone who handles the maintenance of those folks, keeping their saws sharpened (if I can borrow one of Steven Covey's Highly Effective Habits), and challenging them to grow. And they have a program for retention. They retain the good ones, retrain the "okay" ones, and vaporize the bad ones. Yep, vaporizing is important (and honorable). Once in a while even a dud gets through the best hiring screens. A good district, headed toward excellence, has the courage and fortitude to dismiss any employee that can't be retrained, recycled, or repointed in the direction of excellence. We will discuss this in further detail in Chapter Eight, but let's say, for now, that to develop a school of outstanding character it is essential to surround yourself with outstanding characters.

The end never comes

Hiring people of character, constantly training and inspiring them, building on their successes, transferring their energy and passion to a system of character, and doing it all by being the very best administrator possible is a daunting thought. It starts slow, builds momentum, and can explode with positive energy. To see a system infuse a community through positive example and leadership is more exciting than words can describe. The pride that comes from finding and building character flows and glows in each of your "educators" and students. What a reward!

There is no set recipe for accomplishing these goals. It takes collaborative effort, discussion, agreement, compromise, value setting and clarification, planning, and ethical leadership. What starts with baby steps can quickly feel like a championship track meet.

It starts with one person. You. See the possibilities and get others to join the mission. Build character by building characters.

Chapter Seven

Perception is Reality

Jim Burgett

The perfect school always (1) tends to operational and facility details; (2) is organized, neat, clean, and visibly welcoming; (3) is user-friendly and communicates in a professional yet pleasant way; (4) meets or exceeds the expectations of the public that uses it, the students who attend it, and the personnel who manage and work in it; (5) constantly evaluates and measures how it functions; (6) is a visible and real source of community pride, and (7) is perceived as a place of success and vision.

Elsewhere in this book we say that the devil really is in the details. In this chapter we will analyze the perception of your school or school system. That analysis might include calling the office, walking the hallways and campus grounds, testing public relations, even asking others at the bowling alley or market checkout lines. We will see how important it is for any district to truly understand, and handle, public perception as it relates to true reality.

Since the perfect school is an ideal and a goal, to get there we must take the road of excellence. Everybody wants to take that road but when the destination is Perception, it's particularly winding and hilly and has no clear curbs. It requires consistent effort, dedication, and a broad and open perspective. Worse yet, it has sadly been left off of all maps and out of the agenda about educational administration or management.

Lest this topic appear ephemeral or gossameric, however, perception as a critical component in developing the perfect school is as important as curriculum, personnel, and student achievement. This chapter is based on the simple premise that "perception is reality." It can be argued that the premise is too broad or that there is no scientific proof that it is true. In a brick-and-mortar way, I half agree with you. On the other hand, what one perceives is usually what one believes to be true. The perception may be wrong, it may even change, or it may be totally misinterpreted, but no matter, what one perceives usually defines what one believes. And in the perception of a perfect school that is no small thing.

Enough dawdling. How do we apply perceptions to the creation of a perfect school? Let's focus on four areas: what you see, what you experience, what you hear, and what you know.

What you See

Mentally picture a perfect school. It is pleasing to both the eye and mind. Coming up its sidewalk for the first time, you see a place that makes you feel welcome and proud. You might see a building constructed of concrete blocks, wood siding, fancy bricks, or maybe even expensive stone and shiny metal. Whatever the exterior, the perception should be the same: it is clean, neat, cared for, and honored. You see a school house that is treated with respect and is well maintained. It gives you a warm, positive feeling. What might the checklist of the exterior of such a perfect school ask?

- Are the grounds carefully landscaped, neatly trimmed, and well maintained?
- Is the campus safe and inviting?
- Are there appropriate signs telling the visitor where to park?
- Is it clear where you enter the building and how to proceed once you are inside?
- Does the signage make you feel welcome, or is it simply instructive (and cold)?

Not so long ago I went to speak at a well-regarded high school in the suburbs of Chicago. The campus was large, the grounds well manicured, and the parking lots were staffed by guards in small houses. Everything was there except instructions. I had no idea where to park, what door to enter, or how to get into this beautiful edifice. So I drove into a lot, past an empty guard house, and found a parking spot near the back end of the lot. I parked and walked what seemed like a mile until I got to a guard house that was occupied by a pleasant woman.

She very nicely told me that I was in the student lot and needed to move my car to the visitors' lot. She pointed to the visitors' lot; it was as unmarked as the student lot! I walked back to my car, drove to the visitors' lot, and discovered that it was completely full. I then drove back to the guard house, shared my predicament, and was allowed to park in the spot next to the guard house. I was then directed to an entrance door that was again a long, long walk from the lot. When I got to the door, it was locked. This all took place on a school day just a few minutes after classes had begun. I waited a few minutes (I'm not sure why) and then started to hike back to the guard house when I saw another person enter an unmarked door far to my right. I walked there, entered the unlocked door, and was greeted by a lady behind a glass window. She welcomed me, asked my name, and I spent the next five minutes while she cleared my admission into the building. I asked her about the door and she said it was the after-hours entrance once school had begun. I asked her how someone would know that. She said, "I guess you learn it the first time to visit our school." She was very serious. She smiled and we both moved on.

The school was beautiful inside. Well maintained. Clean, bright, and inviting. The staff was friendly and helpful. The signage inside the school was the best I have ever seen. There were signs to each wing, to the offices, to the restrooms, even signs welcoming students and visitors to the school. The inside was an A+. The outside, although a beautiful structure, was a visitor's nightmare. Which of these will I remember longest? My perception was permanently tainted. (I shared my experience with the administration and was assured that things would improve.)

What could they have done to make my first impression almost perfect? Simple. At the very least they could have emailed me a parking and entrance map with the confirmation of my visit. They could have posted large, clear, and informative signs that identified and directed visitors, students, and staff to the appropriate parking lots. They could have clearly identified directions to entrance doors, and then marked those doors. And how about posting signs that read "Need Help? Stop and see our Security Staff at the red security stations." (And then make sure they painted the guard houses red and properly marked them.) They could have a posted sign to use the phone if the security staff member is away from the shelter. This school could have afforded all of these suggestions. But if they couldn't have afforded personal help or outside phone lines, then certainly signage that clearly directs the visitor to the right places would have been important—and appreciated.

Perception is reality. Let's say that the sign on the entrance door said:

"This door is locked when school is in session.
Press the button below for assistance.
All visitors must go the office to be processed."

Here is what might happen. A person might try the door, find that it is locked (it is 9 a.m. on a school day), and just leave. They'd get mad and wouldn't read past the first line. But even if they did read farther and pushed the button, they'd likely hear a release noise. They'd still have to know to open the door—and then start the search for the office. Good intentions but likely a lost or irked visitor.

My first impression would be that the school is, at best, impersonal. I don't feel welcomed, and nothing has been done to make this experience positive. And I don't like to think that soon I must be processed. Isn't bologna processed?

Here's a different solution with a different sign.

"Welcome to Jefferson Jr. High. For the safety of our students, we ask that you push the red button to gain admittance during normal school hours. A member of our office staff will give your further information through the intercom."

In this case, you have provided a welcome, an explanation of why the door is locked, and clear directions of what to expect. The "human" voice can further the positive experience by welcoming the guest to the office or by indicating that someone will be at the door to meet them momentarily. Imagine, a real life person offering a welcome and giving help! What an impressive first experience!

If you are saying that all of this is way too simple, way too logical, and not worthy of several pages in this book, then congratulations. You are one of the few who truly recognizes the importance of a positive and welcoming first impression. Trust me when I tell you that the majority of schools would not get an A on the success of their first impressions. Too many would fail.

When I walk into a school for the first time these are some questions I usually ask:

- Was I able to find the school easily from street signs in the community?
- Is the school clearly marked by name and grade?
- Is there an informative and interesting signboard in front of the school?
- Are the sidewalks and driveways level and safe?
- Is the property well maintained?
- Is the landscaping or property appropriate, neat, and/or unique?
- What will I remember about the outside of the school or the property?
- Are entrances and parking lots clearly labeled and user friendly?
- Once inside the school, do I know and understand security procedures?

- Are the people inside the school proud of their institution? How do I know?
- Do I feel welcomed by staff and students?
- What will I remember most about the people I meet?
- Is the school warm, safe, and inviting?
- When I look up, down, and all around, do I see and sense cleanliness?

What You Experience

Life itself is an experience. It can be divided into a million components that equal the total of our existence. Sound too complex, too involved to manage? Vision is the same way: millions of images yet we see one composite view at a time. The trick is to deal with "manageable hunks." The same is true for what you experience at a school or within a school system. The key to excellence is to analyze things one manageable hunk at a time, and then fix them. Before you know it, you have accomplished a dynamic systemic change!

Excellence, like life, is the total sum of all the parts. No one single thing makes a school excellent, but the sum of many things can. And then there is the attitude that "excellence breeds excellence." It is a way of being, an expected outcome. Let me explain this with two examples.

My first car was a 1955 Studebaker Speedster. Car freaks will know that this was a classic limited edition, a special gem with the capacity for extraordinary speed and comfort. But not mine. Mine was a tiny step above a junker. Yet with a little help from Earl Scheib and some car catalogs, it was transformed into a metallic blue, low-flying, mean growling machine. It also had a sign on the side that said "Give me a ticket." After my brief love life with a car I should have kept, restored, and sold to pay for my kids' college education, I ended up with a simple, four-cylinder, stick shift Ford Falcon station wagon. It was full of options: an AM radio. The car worked, cost next to nothing to operate, and I learned to love it since I could haul friends back and forth from college who would pay for the gas. I replaced several parts on that car, turned the radio up to hide its squeaks and rattles, and knew that when it was below freezing outside, it would only be a few degrees above freezing inside. My expectations were in line with the product; all was good. Did I cry when I traded it in on my first new car? Not a tear. It was semi-dependable, cheap travel. Nothing more, nothing less. Perceptions and reality were in sync.

Over the years I have been fortunate enough to purchase better vehicles. A close friend and long-time school superintendent un-expectedly died on an operating table just months before he was to collect his first retirement check. This sudden death of one of my mentors was enough to convince my wife to have me buy a con-vertible, something I had always wanted to do. Our reasoning: life is unpredictable and the future doesn't always work on our timeta-ble. As a result, I am now driving my third convertible and it is a beauty. I get annoyed if I hear a rattle. I expect good performance. I keep it spotless. It is pristine in appearance. The car company has a reputation for quality, and I expect it. When it is cold outside, now I turn on the heated seats, set the climate control, and expect the car to be 70 degrees ASAP even if I'm in a raging blizzard. I expect excellence from this car, and I do my part to maintain it. I keep it properly serviced and exceptionally clean. Excellence breeds excellence. Expectations, when set high, yield high results.

The second example excludes names to protect the innocent. It's a true story that identifies one of the biggest problems we have in schools with the concept that "perception is reality." That what individuals experience becomes the mindset of reality—for that individual.

It's the story of a new superintendent coming to a district with his own set of perceptions. Within weeks his set of perceptions and the principal's clashed. The principal went to the superinten-dent and reported a broken window on an entrance door to the small gym. You need to picture the door to get the scope of the problem. The building was old and the doors were oak with small panes of wired glass. The window was probably 6 by 9 inches in size. It was not a main door, not even on a main street, but visible from the sidewalk. Possibly a rock from a lawn mower had cracked the glass. The glass was intact, just cracked. It wasn't loose and posed no immediate threat to safety or security. The superintendent asked if the glass could be replaced at the end of summer along with other maintenance projects. The principal said it could, but that it has been his practice to repair or remove any signs of either vandalism or graffiti immediately. The super said that this was a minor problem and could wait. The principal responded that he had tried to view minor problems as major problems and thus avoid bigger issues. The super asked about vandalism and graffiti. The principal responded that they had experienced little to none over the years. The super then repeated that the window could be replaced on the regular summer maintenance schedule.

To the principal, this was not an issue about safety, security, or about appearance. This was an issue about expectations, standards, and perception. To him, the broken window created a perception that the appearance of the building was unimportant. He took pride in the fact that his old (very old) building was clean, neat, and well maintained. A broken window sent the wrong message. Even a little window in a corner door that might be seen by only a few, maybe only by the neighbors. The super was used to big problems and this didn't even register on his radar as a problem, even a small one. Two administrators with two different levels of experience representing two different concepts of perception. The super perceived no problem. The principal perceived both a facility problem and a change in philosophy.

You might be interested to know that the super came to the principal the next day and told him the window would be replaced as soon as possible. He said he learned from their conversation that he could live with little problems that never turned into big problems. The mindset, or perception, of what was important had been clearly shared by the principal and, after he thought about it, made sense to the superintendent. They became good administrative partners and set an example for others.

For things to change, we must all see reality the same way. If administrators and Board members visualize their perfect school differently, they can't work well together pursuing two sets of perfection. If one set of decision makers is satisfied with a different level of reality than another set of decision makers, it becomes hard, if not impossible, to make progress toward any significant change.

Running a school, or school system, requires that all shareowners line up as a team. And even though it may be next to impossible for them to experience everything exactly the same way, they must reach some consensus on what is acceptable and what is not, on what the level of expectation is, and on a way to travel that road to excellence. This effort and understanding must be a key leadership goal of any effective administrator.

We have talked about what you see (visually) and what you experience (intrinsically). Now let's consider how you conceptualize a plan of attack by what you hear.

What You Hear

A wise old sage—fortunately for me, one of my first mentors—was a principal named Bert Murphy. Bert was a seasoned veteran when I was barely a rookie. He was the principal of our biggest rival, but he was a great Dad and I knew that the advice he gave me over the years was as much fatherly as it was educational. He taught me more than he will ever know. One of the things he told me at a junior high basketball game, when I was both the K-8 principal, 7-8 grade boys basketball coach, and half-time teacher, was that you can only hear when you listen.

In the context of the conversation he was telling me that what I heard from parents when I was coaching was a different message than when I was wearing my principal's cap. In other words, you have to *really* listen to hear what is being said at every level and in each unique circumstance. He was talking to a guy in his twenties trying to balance a young family and an overly ambitious teaching assignment who, at the same time, was trying to create a climate of excellence as the school leader. Bert was saying to me, listen to your family when they have needs. Listen to parents and teachers when they share concerns. Listen to your heart and your soul when you sense things aren't right. Listen to the clues and cues that people and situations share no matter what role you are playing and no matter what you personally think and feel. Listen to input. Guess what? As usual, Bert was right. You can only respond to situations if you "hear" them.

So I am going to suggest that you listen to the reality of your school, or school system, as it is being perceived by others. This might be hard to do in some cases because it might make you aware of two things: what you don't know and what you don't want to know.

How do you "hear" about your school? In three practical ways: (1) informal review, (2) survey, and (3) investigation.

The informal review

This one is simple to execute. All it takes is a notebook and some diligence. You simply look and ask. What you see and what you hear is what you write down. If you hear a group of folks talking at a social gathering about the high cost of school fees, you write that down. If you are told by a parent that they were late for an appointment because the school crossing guard didn't allow cars to pass the intersection for a full 10 minutes, you write that down. If you learn that a teacher is upset because they were shocked to see how much money was taken out of their check for health insurance, you write that down. When a student returns to visit you and tells you that they were poorly prepared for college algebra, you write that down. When you hear that the neighboring schools love block scheduling and you are still on a modular scheduling devised when Horace Mann was still alive, you write that down.

When you see an accumulation of dust and dirt on top of the lockers over at Washington Elementary, you write that down.

Each of these examples can be a story in itself. Let's share just one example.

A tenured, top-rank teacher stomped into my office after school one day. She was steaming mad, which was way out of character for her. She slapped her first paycheck of the year on my desk. She had received it the day before and had waited to come and talk to me. (If she had waited in order to cool down, I was sure glad she hadn't come the day before!) She wanted to know why, after the new contract provided more than a 4% raise, her check was significantly smaller than it was last year! She specifically asked what kind of *tricks* we were playing with "their" money, *again*! I too was a bit perplexed until I gave it some thought. Then I asked her if she was still a member of the teacher's association. This time I think I saw a bit of real steam actually puff out of her ears. "What does that have to do with anything?" she asked. I asked if she had received a copy of the contract settlement last spring after the teachers had settled. She said no and then explained that the union (I prefer to call it a professional association) did not send nonmembers any information. I then told her that part of the new contract was that teachers would be paid twice a month rather than once a month, and this was only half of her monthly salary. Her face turned redder than a St. Louis Cardinal cap. "Oh" was all she could mutter as she quickly fled.

The entry in my notebook said the following: teachers feel we play tricks with their salary. The Association does not notify nonmembers of contract changes. JB (me) failed to mention the change from one check to two in the summer letter. Immediate information needs to be sent to all teachers.

I crafted an email and sent a hard copy to every teacher that very afternoon. It went something like this:

Dear Teaching Staff:

I can only imagine that when you opened your first check this year you were shocked! But when you remembered that you will now be receiving two checks each month, instead of one, you were pleasantly surprised! Just as a reminder, last spring we successfully agreed on a three-year contract that included a 4.2% average increase this year (yours may be higher or lower depending on where you are on the schedule) and even higher increases the next two years. The Board was pleased to agree to this settlement and still maintain a balanced budget. Your Association members did an outstanding job representing all of you during the process.

I want to encourage any teacher to contact me at any time if you have questions about salary, benefits, or the contract. The worst situation is when you don't understand or have unanswered questions. The contract may seem long and confusing to you, but it really is rather clear and easy to understand. I know that the leadership of the district's Professional Association would be happy to help any staff member understand the contract as well.

Have a great year and thanks for the difference you make. I look forward to seeing you in the classroom giving our kids the best education ever.

Jim

What did this letter do? It immediately corrected an oversight. It gave the Association a well deserved pat on the back. It reminded teachers that they have two more years of salary increases. It said we have an open door to any questions. And it ended with a heartfelt note of appreciation.

Keeping open to informal, 24/7 interviews makes a difference. In this case I heard, I listened, I acted. The reality someone had perceived was not indeed reality. Hopefully the new perception put us more on track toward excellence.

Remember this important consideration: every time you correct an incorrect perception, and you do it with class and appropriate procedures, you move one step closer to perfection. Every time.

Survey

Surveys can be complicated mathematical conglomerations that only a grad student taking doctoral statistics can decipher; they can be direct, short, and easy to understand, or they can be somewhere in between. If you are near a university, they often can provide survey assistance. They can help you plan, write, collect, and interpret the survey and data. You can also hire a formal statistical data collection company to help you do the same, usually for big bucks. Or you can send out simple surveys for specific reasons and do your own interpretations. No matter how you do it, surveys can be a wonderful way of measuring perceptions.

In one district I am aware of, two months after school starts, they mail a transportation survey to every family in the district, even if the student doesn't ride the bus. The survey asks simple questions to bus riders like:

- Is your bus on time?
- According to your student, how do you rate the behavior on the bus?
- Do you have any concerns about the safety of your student's bus ride to and from school?

For those whose kids do not ride the bus, other questions are asked like:

- From your discussion with other parents, how do you rate the safety of our bus system?
- Would you like to see transportation services expanded?

In both surveys plenty of opportunity is given for additional comments.

The surveys are collected by the main office, screened to make sure that nothing inappropriate is written, and then reviewed by a panel of representatives from the bus company, central office administration, driver training team, and drivers. The surveys are used to evaluate the system; the meeting is an opportunity to outline ways to improve the system. This process has resulted in numerous communication procedure improvements, training program changes, upgrades in safety standards, etc. The goal each year is to receive better marks and more positive comments. About a month after the surveys are mailed, a follow-up letter is sent to all families (or is included in the district newsletter) that acknowledges the survey, talks about changes, and thanks the participants. This provides timely feedback and shows that the survey is taken seriously and that the district wants to improve.

Another district, during two three-week periods each year, hands every third visitor to the main office a stamped envelope with a survey inside that asks about their visit. The person handing out the survey asks each recipient to mail it back by the end of the next day, if possible. The survey asks a number of questions such as:

- How easy was it to locate the main office?
- If you are visiting for the first time, what is your first impression?
- Would you please rate your waiting wait time, service rendered, attitude of staff, office climate, etc.?

The less gracious might say that the office does its very best job during these three weeks That might be true, but how many offices have anything like this which makes the staff even think about their service? Imagine, for six weeks a year the main office concentrates on doing a better job. That has to make a difference.

Surveys are easy to create, simple to distribute, and can provide a plethora of information if they are used and valued. I especially like staff surveys that ask open-ended questions such as:

- If I could change one thing that would make this a better place for student learning I would......
- The one thing that I appreciate the most about the people I work with at Lincoln Elementary is.......

- What are five changes you think could help our school earn an overall rating of excellence by our parents and other taxpayers....

These are questions that make a person think. Of course you get some goofy responses, but all in all you will see a trend if a trend is apparent, or it will open your eyes to new areas of concern that you might not be the slightest bit aware of.

Surveys take time; if used correctly, they can help improve reality.

Investigation

This is one of the most unique and helpful ways to measure perception. Hire someone to do an investigative evaluation of your district. I suggest another administrator who knows little, if anything, about your school or school system. Someone who won't be recognized in your district. And someone you trust.

Have him or her come and register a "family," check your website, call your offices, attend a baseball game, and eat at the local restaurant and ask lots of questions. Suggest they get a haircut by a local barber or visit a local hair salon and ask about the school, acting as a prospective community member. Then ask them to compile a confidential score card of sorts along with recommendations. Have them report on the perceptions of the district's academic offerings, the success of student achievement, the ease of locating the schools, the "service rating" when they made cold calls to the offices, the helpfulness when they visited a school guidance counselor to register their four kids, one of whom (for example) has special needs. Have them report on what real estate agents said about the district, what the banker said, what the lady on the street and the guy in the pharmacy had to say. And then have them list their own first impressions. What did they think when they walked down that hallway toward the office in the high school the first time? Was it dark, dirty, inviting, warm, enchanting, gloomy? Why?

I have done this very service for some of my associates and the results were amazing. The super and his staff learned a great deal by my surprise visit and comprehensive follow-up report. It can be an awesome experience, but you must be ready for a reality check—or at least a perceived reality check!

How do you initiate such an investigation? Meet with the person you want to perform the investigation, offsite. Agree on a reasonable fee for several full days of work, and request a written report plus a detailed, face-to-face discussion. Agree in advance if the report is partially or entirely confidential. In one experience, I had to report to the superintendent that I thought an administrator I met with after lunch smelled like he had been drinking. It was an observation only and could have been a sticky legal issue. Subsequent follow-up investigations, based on my observation, resulted in the discovery that the administrator was a closet alcoholic. He was offered assistance the next year and given a leave. He resigned a short time later. Confidentiality is an issue if an investigation is to be meaningful. Ask the investigator to list the good with the bad, the areas of needed improvement along with the areas that are impressive, and then let him or her do the job, without you knowing when or even how. Believe me, this is a very effective tool if you are serious about getting on that road to excellence.

What you know

It finally comes down to what you know. If you have looked, experienced, and listened, if you have surveyed, asked, and investigated, and if you have seriously tried to find out what others perceive your school or school system to be, then you have completed the most important phase of change. You know what needs to be done. You can hard copy specific things to make your learning institution better, but what you know is meaningless if you don't act on it. It is no different than going to the doctor, sharing your symptoms, taking the tests, being scanned and X-rayed and probed and measured... You find out exactly what your condition is. Then you go home and die because you did nothing with the information.

If your car stalls and sputters at every stop sign, you get it fixed.

Sometimes what you know needs to be translated so you know precisely what to do. But then it's time for action. Every step you take to correct one unwarranted perception is a step toward excellence. That is the point of this chapter, and it is an important one.

What is worse then a poorly operating district where kids don't learn what they could learn, people don't respect each other, and the public doesn't support the schools? It's a group of administrators who know the problems and don't try to fix them.

If you know what needs to be done, do it. I like the FBI concept of forming BAM teams when they have a serious situation. BAM means "by any means." Sometimes we need to consider BAM teams at schools. Solve the problem with creative and energetic enthusiasm. Fix each component that you see, hear, feel, and know, one at a time, with collaboration, teamwork, and passion. The more you fix, the better the perception and the better the reality will be.

Summary

This element of the perfect school is probably the most inclusive and complex. It involves a dedicated review of details, of communication, of facilities, and of all things that leave an impression on the public. But it's more than public relations or communications. It is a climate of 24/7 observation, adjustment, correction, and change. To work, it will take a staff of people who are willing to evaluate, question, investigate, and review the operations of all aspects of the program and institution. It will take a leader who is willing to set expectations and then be sure they are met and understood. The road to excellence pitted with troublesome details can quickly get potholes of frustration. Fixing the details keeps the road smooth and easy to travel.

E.B. White, the humorist and writer, wrote "I arise in the morning torn between a desire to improve the world, and a desire to enjoy the world." I love that attitude. I also think you can enjoy the world while you improve it. Once you see a group of educators get excited about the road to excellence, once you see the community develop a level of real pride for their schools, and once you realize that kids truly are learning in a caring and special environment, then you too will understand that striving for the perfect school can be one of the most rewarding goals of your life. And you will wake up every morning with a passion to reach that goal.

Chapter Eight

Eliminate the Weakest Link

Jim Burgett

The perfect school (1) hires and motivates excellent employees, (2) adopts an understandable evaluation process, (3) makes sure all employees understand their purpose in the organization, (4) clearly communicates and consistently raises expectations, (5) remediates performance that does not meet expectations, (6) terminates for either poor performance traits or attitudes or (7) terminates weak employees, and (8) at all levels, in all job categories, eliminates the weakest links.

The importance of hiring, contracting, and working with the best is the foundation of this chapter. We will explore hiring practices, mentoring, evaluation, and expectations of all personnel. We will also see that "elimination" is a very important step toward developing the perfect school. We will focus on how to replace weakness with strength and what it takes to build a staff of outstanding employees.

The Long and Winding Road to Excellence

Chapter 6 of this book talks about building a work force with character. It discusses the often neglected art of elimination, or removal of personnel that have not, or possibly cannot, achieve excellence. Dumping the characters and replacing them with a staff of character. Is this a swift process? Hardly. It may take years to filter out the nonproductive, ineffective, burned out or pooped out deadwood that dams the stream flowing to perfection. But when you read this chapter, you will see that it can and should be done.

> "Building human capital may not get headlines, like opening a slew of new schools or completely redesigning a district's curriculum, but veterans of urban education reform say it is one of the key behind-the-scenes factors in determining if changes succeed or fail ..."[1]

Carl Vogel

I like the phrase "building human capital." Nothing is more important than the quality of people who compose our school systems. Notice that I didn't limit this to teachers or administrators. Every human being who works in a school system is fundamental to the success of that system. Every one. And this, to me, is one of the most neglected components of the race to excellence.

So what you are about to read must be thought of in two very important ways. First, the process of producing a staff of excellent employees takes time. Sometimes a very long time. Second, no one is excluded from the process.

Why So Long to Build an Exceptional Staff?

Why is this a long process? The answer is simple. We seldom have the chance to build a new school system from scratch. We almost always start at point A and work toward point B. Point A is an existing system that we hope to modify and move toward perfection. That means we need to take what we have and then tweak, alter, improve, change, or produce something that fits the system's "new" expectations and goals. Alas, it isn't always possible. Some employees won't bend without breaking. Some won't see or embrace the new objectives. Some simply won't be motivated to improve. Some, to be honest, will need to make way for others.

Evaluations, improvement plans, systemic changes, remediation, and other legal hoops all take time to process. Each state will

---

[1] "The New Urban Legend," *District Administrator*, November, 2005.

pose a different set of procedures that must be followed to ensure that every employee is treated fairly and with respect. Some of these steps take months, some take years. Some are clear and easy to follow, some are ridiculously cumbersome and lengthy. But no matter what, the end goal must remain prominently in sight: the employment of people willing to work toward a perfect school system. Why does it take so long to clean house and end up with a staff of excellence? Because in some cases you need to say "so long" to current staff and replace them with well-trained and highly productive folks.

Process and Procedure

It is not the intent of this book to tell you how to follow the dictates of your state or your district. Most states require that the school have, or follow, an approved teacher/employee evaluation program. Then, if necessary, to follow guidelines for remediation or improvement. Finally, if needed, to pursue specific steps for dismissal or reassignment. Certified staff are often handled in a rather legalistic manner. Non-certified staff generally have fewer barriers to overcome, but enough to make the job challenging. Unfortunately for school administrators, some states handle contractual employees, such as bus drivers, kitchen staff, or custodians, differently. The guidelines covering hiring, development, and dismissal may be in the hands of the contractor rather than the school. This creates a problem when the school is trying to make sure that every employee meets similar standards of excellence. In situations like these the district must ensure that hiring, training, and dismissal practices follow similar guidelines and expectations as used with district-managed employees.

The System is Part of the Solution

No process should be adapted or approved unless everyone understands the ultimate goals of the program. "Everyone" means every person from the Board to the evaluated employee. There should be no confusion that the process being used is there for one of two reasons—to improve or remove. Some more politically correct types will shudder at this statement. "To remove?" they gasp! Yep, that is the secondary purpose of evaluation. The primary purpose is to improve. If the person can't improve, he or she must go. The politically insecure will reply, "But what if the person is doing a fine job, doesn't need improvement, and already gets the highest ratings possible?"

My answer? That's impossible. No one can get the highest rating possible in everything. There is always something they can do better. If they are the very best bus driver, teacher, or superintendent you have ever experienced, then their talents should be tapped to train others and their "score card" should be expanded to include new challenges, like ways to improve the quality of other bus drivers or how to reach new and uncharted levels of expectations. The evaluation should include a discussion of how the top-rated educator can expand the profession. If they are unwilling to improve, even beyond the A+ level of achievement, then you need to ask how far they can travel on the new road to excellence.

The evaluation plan is not the answer. It is only part of the solution to improve your staff. No matter which of several highly successful and worthy plans a district adopts, it will only be successful if everyone involved:

1. Understands the goals of the process
2. Is properly trained in the process, and
3. Uses the process to move the system toward excellence

At the time of this writing teacher evaluation systems, such as those used in Toledo, Ohio, or Rochester, New York, are leading the way in teacher-employee development, evaluation, and improvement. An entire book could be written on evaluation plans and procedures. In fact, they have been. That is not the issue here. The issue is the intent. Everyone must understand that the intent of all evaluations is to improve or remove.

Evaluation Leads to Training

It matters not which program of evaluation or remediation a school system utilizes. Every system can be successful if all participants buy into the goals and understand the desired outcomes. To change behavior will take training; often it is aggressive and lengthy. An example is the process that the Ritz-Carlton does to train all of its employees—all of them—on their basic 20 service principles that I mentioned in Chapter 5. They meet with everyone, every day, and during each month they review the 20 basic premises. They read them, discuss how to implement them, talk about successes and difficulties, and offer ways to improve them. Every day, every employee. The training never ends. A system that is working toward perfection must understand that employee improvement is not a one-stop process, but a long-term commitment to regular and meaningful training.

Traditions

Let's think about traditional teacher evaluations. New teachers may (or may not) get some limited training in how the evaluation, improvement, and performance process works. Then they get evaluated. During their first year of teaching they may be evaluated one, two, three, or four times. Then the evaluations come less frequently. Teachers aren't stupid. They prepare for the evaluation session, often selecting a comfortable lesson, getting a good night's sleep, and then "performing" to the best of their abilities when the evaluator is present. It is similar to the bus driver who sees the supervisor coming with her/his clipboard. They make sure every step on the pre-trip inspection form is carefully completed, then they greet and talk with students in an unusually polite manner. Everyone knows that an evaluation made under these conditions borders on being totally bogus.

How many times have you heard an administrator comment on the poor performance of an employee with the full understanding that their "official" job evaluations are acceptable? Everyone knows why. Probably the contract only allows for an evaluation review to be "booked" in a formal, predictable manner. So "C" employees, or worse, slip by once again. Kids, and the system, pay the price.

Evaluate, Remediate, Eliminate

Every evaluation process should be based on these three steps. Evaluate the performance on a "real time" basis. Remediate anything that doesn't lean toward excellence or improvement. Eliminate the weak performance areas or eliminate the employee from the payroll. Harsh? Maybe. Necessary? Absolutely.

A recent report indicated that there are approximately 6,000,000 total staff members working in the public schools in the United States.[2]

If 10% of that six million are doing a poor job, that is 600,000 people. Even if 99% of the total were doing a great job, and I mean really doing a great job, that would still mean 60,000 would be hindering their schools or hurting the kids. I suggest that no district can afford to have *one* employee on the payroll who isn't traveling on the road of excellence. The cost to our kids is too great.

That said, let's emphasize the importance of an evaluation system that has at its core the goals of improvement or removal.

The New Agenda

NCLB and other efforts for school reform almost always include a call for higher quality teachers and principals. But what about support staff? What about school secretaries? What about hall monitors or play ground supervisors? What about the school treasurer or the maintenance personnel? Shouldn't everyone who is in the system be of "high quality" and trained to understand the goals and visions of the district?

We talked about the Ritz-Carlton in the chapter about service. Let's revisit that example for a moment. The guy you see planting annuals on the hillside, the lady who changes the sheets, the young girl parking cars, the person behind the desk—every single person who works for the company—understands the credo, the mission, and the vision of the corporation and of their venue. They understand that if they aren't in line with the RC direction and goals, they won't remain employed there. They also understand that if they accept the challenges and do their part to provide the best service in the best way possible, they will enjoy the benefits of personal and professional improvement.

---

[2] *Public Elementary and Secondary Students, Staff, Schools, and School Districts: School Year 2003-04*, National Center for Education Statistics; see at www.nces.ed.gov.

It's more than a corporate process, it becomes a part of who they are and why they are there. That example is the essence of this chapter. It is not about what checklist you use; rather, it's about owned expectations for improvement and excellence.

Michael Shiber, Superintendent at Rockford, Michigan, reported in an interview that one of the keys to the success in his district was continuous improvement.[3] One of his secrets was a monthly meeting with support staff and the teacher's association. "We resolve issues before they become problems." He reports that in his last 14 years he has not had a grievance and most of the time they settle contracts in days rather than weeks.

Eliminating the weakest link can only be done by identifying the weakest link. Continual discussion, goal setting, evaluation, and character development help any good administrator identify the areas of need and the weakest providers.

Let's look at four steps that help identify the weak links in any organization.

1. Clarify the purpose
2. Communicate the expectations
3. Set goals
4. Evaluate, remediate, terminate

Clarify the Purpose

Recently I was asked to meet with the administrators and Board of Education of a district to talk about developing a strategic plan. When the superintendent called to present the specifics of the process to his Board, he also asked me to somehow talk to the Board members about micromanaging. He shared with me several horror stories of how two of the members (one the President) were weak and manipulative. One had a spouse who was a teacher and the spouse was a constant "leak" to her husband about teachers who used the Internet during class, came to work late, and were out of the classroom during instructional times. The other Board member just wanted to run the place, even to dictating the wording

---

[3] Schater, Ron, "Integrity, Accountability, Continuity," *District Administration*, August, 2006.

on newsletters that went home to parents. The superintendent felt that the walls were closing in and, had he not already planned to retire at the end of the year, he would be looking for a new job.

I asked him some simple questions after doing an attentive job of listening:

1. Do you think you would be rehired if you were not already going to retire?
2. How do you rate the other five Board members?
3. What percentage of your staff is doing a good job?
4. Can you list positive things your school has accomplished?

Here were his responses:

1. I would probably be rehired 7-0 or 6-1.
2. Four are excellent, one is learning and could be an excellent Board member. Only two are problems, and of those one may be salvageable.
3. At least 90% are excellent teachers.
4. No problem! We have a long list of accomplishments that I can easily write and share with you. (He then proceeded to tell me many of them, with great enthusiasm.)

This administrator demonstrated what plagues most organizations: a small percentage of negatives are allowed to dominate the large percentage of positives. It is like the teacher who keeps the entire class in from recess because one or two kids were late, or laughed, or threw a wad of paper. You get the idea.

Focus on the Positive

Most of the time those who cause the most problems do it because they don't understand their role or the purpose of their position. Do Board members who micromanage understand the role of an individual Board member? Have they undergone appropriate training? Has anyone told them that they have no power as an individual and can only act when functioning as a Board? Has anyone shared the chain of command? Has there been a meeting to talk about the issues, the frustrations, and the situation? Maybe an outsider is needed. Maybe a session at a conference on Boardmanship should be scheduled. Maybe a lunch with the Board member to clarify what you both think the job is—or should be.

The administrator of this district in the example needed to focus on two things: (1) Two Board members and (2) 10% of the staff. A good way to do that is by confirming the good that is happening and that the good things are helping the school or system reach its collective purpose. Focusing on what is right is a good way to steer everyone in a positive direction. Allowing the negatives to rule the actions and thoughts diverts the positive energy that is needed to travel the road of excellence.

Turning it Around

To be more specific with the superintendent, I suggested that he call the wayward Board president and ask him to meet him for lunch, but that the superintendent and Board member first jot down their thoughts on his role or purpose as both a Board member and as president. At lunch they could compare notes. If the Board president asked why, the answer should be simple. Tell her that in order to best meet the needs of kids you feel that you need to be sure you are both on the same page. Don't get into the discussion on the phone, wait until you can compare notes.

The next step is simple. Stay positive. Bring that list of accomplishments. Talk about how good you feel about it. Thank the Board president for serving. Focus on moving forward. Then ask for the Board president to share her thoughts on what she thinks her purpose is. Then share yours. The goal is to find the areas you agree on and write them down. Focus on the positive first. Then talk about the areas where you disagree and try to get a conversation going about why and how you can reach common ground.

Rocket Science?

Nope, this isn't rocket science. This is basic Communications 101. This is also not that easy to do well. The alternative is to do nothing, complain about the problem, let it fester and possibly explode, or hope it will go away. Another alternative is to avoid the issue, count the days until retirement (or the next job), and take a detour off the road of excellence. The perfect school? Forget it. Unless you are willing to focus on the problems at hand, they will remain a roadblock to success.

Sometimes they will go away. I remember a Board member who was a real, certified, registered, licensed pain in the butt. I think he was born negative. He caused the positive momentum of a district to slow down. If he'd had his way, every good decision made would have had to have been rethought. And then, all of a sudden, he stopped being a pain and became neutral. His attendance became sporadic; his interest waned. Marital problems took center stage and his negativity was focused on another target. Sadly, his personal losses (divorce and separation from family) became our gain. (One wonders, if he had been turned around as a Board member, would that have had a positive effect on his personal life?)

Problems exist at every level. A teacher with a bad attitude about the dress code. A janitor who can't stand the guy who comes in for the night shift so he fails to communicate properly, if at all. A cook who yells at kids who forget to put their silverware in the right tray. A bus driver who does a full inspection only when he is being inspected. A teacher's aide who shares confidential information about some of the parents of the special needs kids she works with. Every one of those situations needs to be fixed. Every one of those people needs to understand the purpose of their job and the importance of doing it well. Every one of those examples is a roadblock in the quest for excellence.

Communicate the Expectations

It is essential that every employee understands the purpose and importance of his or her role in the system. I was once addressing a group of office employees and I randomly went through the audience asking a handful what they did. One lady said she literally worked in a converted closet and counted money all day. She said she only saw kids on her way to and from her "cell," as she jokingly called her work area. I asked her if she thought her job was important. Her response was, "I guess so, but anyone could do it with a little training." I loved her answer. My response to it was simple and short. I told her that all jobs require training, but if people didn't do their jobs well the system wouldn't work. Counting money correctly is the baseline for the accounting department. Everything that has to do with accounting—budgets, audits, paychecks, invoices, financial records, funding—is based on correct financial records. It is the foundation of the operations of the district. It all starts in her cell. If she messed up, if she was dishonest, if she put money in the wrong accounts, if she made any error for any reason, she could jeopardize the entire reputation and operation of the district. Before I was done I had the audience thinking that our national economy was in the hands of this woman. I concluded by saying "You are not only important, you are essential!"

Later, at a break, she came up to me, a bit emotional, and told me that she never felt so important. She even admitted that often at school she felt like the unloved stepsister. She thanked me for using her as an example.

That is what every employee needs to feel. Important, relevant, meaningful, filling a needed purpose! You can't realistically raise expectations if employees don't feel that the service they perform has value. When you multiply zero by anything you get zero. You have to establish a value, and then you can raise it with higher expectations.

If the money lady feels valued and important it will be easier to tell her you have found a new software program that will allow her to handle additional responsibilities and become even more involved with the school's financial program. If she understands her purpose and knows her value, you can adjust the expectations of her job with ease.

Set Expectations Carefully

Setting expectations can make the good better and the weak stronger. Expectations are the cornerstone to improvement. Higher AYPs, better scores on the Stanford, a higher percentage of students enrolled in the Ag Department, more solo and ensemble contest winners, a higher graduation rate, improved rating by the Health Department, fewer bus accidents, whatever the expectations are, setting them is the first and most important step in reaching them. They have to be understood, owned, and cooperatively established to have value.

People need to know that to travel the road of excellence in pursuit of perfection, there must be excellence at every turn. The expectation of excellence has to be real.

Set Goals

Expectations lead to goals. John is a second-year eighth grade math teacher. The school where he works has succeeded in meeting the state standards for eighth grade math for the past five years, but the percentage of students meeting the standards has dropped slightly the last two years. The school and math department have agreed that the expectations for achievement in math need to be raised. Just meeting the standards is acceptable, but not excellent, so the expectation has been elevated. That's a good first step. Now John and his fellow math teachers have been asked to set specific goals to reach the new level of expectation. John's principal realizes that after only one full year of teaching John is still a rookie and may need some help not only in setting the goals but achieving them.

So the principal decides to divide the six eighth grade math teachers into three teams of two, and pairs John with Alice, a 32-year veteran who is also a National Board Certified teacher. Alice and John don't know each other very well. John would probably have preferred to be paired with Jordan who has been teaching math for 12 years, at several grade levels, and who coaches basketball with John. But Jordan is teamed with Larry, another veteran who is a master at delivery and a very successful motivator of kids. Jordon is a good technician, but not an exciting teacher. The principal is not only helping these teachers work on setting appropriate goals to reach the new achievement expectations, but is also using the pairing process to strengthen individual skills. John will learn some of the tools that Nationally Board Certified teachers learn in their training. Jordan might learn some teaching techniques that could make his delivery more exciting and more productive. The principal has asked Alice and Larry to work with John and Jordan by sharing their special talents. Who wins? Everyone. Alice and Larry feel honored to be recognized as talented teachers. John and Jordan will reap the benefits of excellent role models. Meaningful goals will be set. Most important, kids will get better instruction.

Evaluate, Remediate, Terminate

Here we are again, the keys to ensuring a high quality staff. Find an evaluation program that helps define the purpose of each employee and the expectations of the job, as well as measures how well the employee meets the stated goals. If the evaluation indicates that the employee is not meeting the standards of the system, then you need to fix the problem (remediate). Fixing the problem may be as minor as a small adjustment in skill level, knowledge, or delivery methods or as large as a full remediation plan as outlined by the policies of the district or legal mandates.

The Pitfall of Remediating

Remediating at its fullest, most intimidating level needs to be entered with one initial goal, to elevate the performance of the employee to standards that warrant retention in the position. Remediating may not provide, or even promote, excellence. It may only ensure "meeting standards" as opposed to exceeding them. Remediating is not always the best ingredient to getting on the road to excellence, but it's a necessary step if you want to get to the entrance ramp. It's like a basal reader. You have to master the reader before you pick up a novel. Remediating may take a harmful employee and give him the opportunity to become a helpful one. However, you must pass "neutral" before you head toward excellence. And that brings up the pitfall. Many administrators will remediate a poor employee and bring her to an acceptable level, but stop there. They either assume that the employee can't do better or they are happy the complaints have stopped, the work ethic has improved, the kids are at least getting an "average" opportunity, or the safety, cleanliness, or general atmosphere of the school or system is no longer in jeopardy. They accept that as a workable solution. But who just wants mediocrity? Stopping there accepts the average, the bland. To achieve continual improvement, to travel the road of excellence, remediation can't be your last stop.

The Final Frontier: Termination

Does that mean you move on to "termination"? Yes, but termination has two avenues. You can terminate the employee: displace, fire, relocate, eliminate. Or you can terminate their average attitude, mediocre performance, or award-winning dullness. Terminate those behaviors and replace them with exceptional ones. Move the borderline employee not just over the edge of acceptance but into the territory of exceptional performance.

So how do you terminate bad performance?

There are many ways to eliminate negative performance. Sincere and meaningful professional development is a start. A janitor who can't clean may need to attend a series of cleaning skill workshops. A bus driver who had the personality of Jason in the Halloween movies may need to participate in some discipline workshops, or attend a class in adolescent behavior. A well-trained teacher that has no skill in motivation may need to attend an academy on teaching environment.

Or, you could pair up two employees who can share skills or techniques and do some in-house training. Formal training or informal opportunities, personal conferences, self-evaluation, looking at teaching tapes of others or themselves, or reviewing professional training series are just a few of the options available. The Toledo Plan is a formal method of remediating new teachers. It is a collaborative attempt to get them on the track to excellence. It represents a partnership that exists in some districts between the school and the associations to work toward improvement. It works though an intervention-type process. It is one of dozens of ways to replace poor work traits with good ones.

And how do you terminate bad employees?

Every school or system should have a formal plan for termination. Evaluate, remediate, and—if remediation fails—terminate. That is the normal process most schools use. The key is the honest and sincere effort to remediate. If it doesn't work, then get rid of the employee.

If the remediation process is not totally successful and you end up with an average teacher, rather than an excellent one, you still need to work on "terminating" their average qualities and moving them toward excellence. Do you fire them? Not if they are meeting "OK" standards and "passing" evaluations. But you can raise the bar. You can set newer and higher expectations. You can say that average isn't good enough. You can sit down and tell them that they simply are not good enough for the new program, the new direction, the new drive for excellence. An honest talk with a new set of expectations may be all that is needed to get the teacher to jump to another district, another job, or another position in the system. It may lead to creative ways to accelerate retirement or promote a career change. If done in a positive manner that takes into consideration legal parameters and the best interest of the employee, in most cases you can make a change. It may mean a buyout, a transfer, or help with a career change. It may mean several meetings working with the association or it may mean setting new expectations.

Here are some certainties about removing an employee who is average but not excellent:

It may be difficult, but it is possible.
It may take time, but the result is worth it.
It may cost money, but in the long run it will save.
It may take creativity, but that is good.
It should be a win-win for employee and school.
It will be a win-win for students and staff.

Excuses, Excuses

Over the years I have heard every excuse for not terminating an employee. It costs too much. There are too many legal hoops to jump through. They will sue you. It isn't the right thing to do for the employee. They will retire in a few years so why bother. They aren't hurting anyone. They are doing the best they can. Their heart is in the right place.

Here are my answers: An employee that prevents a system from providing the best opportunities for kids is costing kids a chance to learn. Hoops are made to jump through. Go through the process once and everyone will know you will do it again. You can be sued for anything, so why fear being sued for doing what is best for kids? You are here for the kids, not the employee. Every year that you give an employee a pass because they are close to retirement, or because they aren't hurting someone, or because they have a good heart is a year you deny a student the opportunity to get the best education you can provide.

Termination is more of a choice than an act. Once you decide that you can't bring the employee any farther, that they are preventing the system from attaining excellence, and that you have given remediation your very best effort, then make the choice to terminate and find a way.

The sooner you eliminate the weakest links, the faster you speed down the road of excellence. It's worth the work. It really isn't an option if you want a perfect school.

The word "impossible" is not in my dictionary.

Napoleon I (1769-1821)

Chapter Nine

The Devil is in the Details

Jim Rosborg

The perfect school (1) sees the influence of legislation and case law on the management of schools, (2) recognizes the importance of outstanding individuals in the learning environment, (3) celebrates educational success, (4) works to make *all* students successful citizens, while digging to find each student's strengths, (5) embraces accountability, and (6) constantly strives to improve curriculum and instruction.

The opening chapter explained the rationale, and some of the difficulties, of defining and implementing "The Perfect School"—goals long sought yet forever elusive. Education leaders have been looking at ways to improve schools since before *McGuffey's Readers*. Today, they have been joined in that quest by others from government, the media, and industry.

We can't discuss the perfect school in a vacuum, nor can we fail to address the impact that current efforts, mostly by the government, have had through such studies and legislation as *A Nation at Risk*, the NCATE, IDEA, and the No Child Left Behind Act. So that will be the focus of this chapter: how they have helped define the current state of education, how they would improve (perhaps, in their view, even "perfect") it, and some of the shortcomings their attempts have created or highlighted.

The three of us writing this book have seen a blizzard of changes aimed at improving the educational outcomes of students we all want to help. Alas, most of those attempts to change have had good intentions but limited results.

Change is a bedrock concept in education. Glenn Brasel, 91, once told me that change will occur many times in one's educational career—often the same change! For example, we went from an academic and assessment approach (when I was attending school) in the 1960s to a humanistic approach in the 1970s, where we had to give reasons why we were teaching basic concepts that stressed individualized instruction. Then when government leaders felt test scores were declining in the early 1980s, we headed back to stress academics and assessment. Now it's said that we're assessing students too much and we should use more individualized instruction. Change is here to stay!

So let's look at practical ways to not only improve the testing results of today's youth, but also to look far beyond testing and assessment. The goal is to provide the framework to develop not only good school citizens but also good and productive lifelong citizens in our society.

To be able to do that, in this book we will discuss the perfect school setting, the perfect teacher and staff, the perfect parent, and the perfect principal. We will also see how perceptions truly lead to reality and how character development is imperative to achieving those goals. We will identify current problems and offer positive solutions, all to help the student.

We feel that dramatic improvements can take place in our current educational system. Not only are we going to consider frequently discussed items such as funding, discipline, assessment, and professional development, we are also going to look at issues such as connecting with students, staff relationships, teacher morale, effective communication, parental involvement, community service, and the development of a curriculum that is carefully planned to maintain student interest by providing a variety of offerings in a focused environment. Finally, while we describe the perfect school, we must also look at long-term problems that have emerged in the American educational system.

We cannot fully tell the story of today's educational system without touching some of the historical implications that shaped current ideologies.

A Nation at Risk

One of greatest educational documents of the past century was a U.S. Government publication titled *A Nation at Risk*, published in 1983 during President Reagan's administration. The study concluded that the American educational system urgently needed immediate and long-term improvement. Some of the recommendations provided in the report have actually been put into place. For example, those commissioned recommended that state and local high school graduation requirements be strengthened to include more requirements in English, reading, mathematics, science, social studies, computer science, and foreign language. One need not look far from where they currently live to find a State Legislature that has enacted new laws regarding more stringent high school requirements. We agree with those goals, as long as the rules do not totally impede programs such as vocational education, fine and practical arts, and physical development.

Let me share an example. When I taught in the '70s and '80s, I had three students who would later become sub-contractors on the house my wife and I built in the early 1990s. When those three were my students at the junior high level, all were struggling in reading and mathematics. In today's society, they probably would not have met or exceeded state standards. When they went to high school, they enrolled in the vocational and technical program. When these same lads appeared as sub-contractors on our house, each one of them was highly skilled in his respective vocational area. They are also successful citizens in our community. Moreover, when we were building our house, each was earning more money than me! Because of the breadth of the U.S. education system, these three men who might not have met or exceeded state standards in the 21st Century were given the tools to succeed.

The second category of recommendations under *A Nation at Risk* was that schools, colleges, and universities adopt more rigorous and measurable standards. Attempts have been made to ensure that this was going to happen through the No Child Left Behind Act (which was signed into law in 2002) and current NCATE (National Council for Accreditation of Teacher Education) standards, which were also developed the same year. In the 2002 edition of their professional standards, NCATE stated that their accreditation determines whether or not schools, colleges, and departments of education meet "demanding standards" for the preparation of professional educators. These requirements are an attempt to establish high standards and to improve the educational process as recommended by the original *A Nation at Risk* study in 1983.[1]

Debate still takes place at the collegiate level regarding the current structuring of the standards movement and how far we will extend it. Dr. Randy Dunn, State Superintendent of Schools in Illinois as this chapter is written, made an interesting observation while speaking to one of my graduate education classes in curriculum in October, 2005. Dr. Dunn asked the students the question that is being asked at colleges and universities throughout the nation. "If you were representing the personnel department of a college or university, which of these two candidates would you hire to be a professor at your institution? The first candidate is world-renowned Nobel Prize winner in English but has little knowledge of current NCATE (collegiate) standards needed for accreditation. The second candidate has had a rather routine instructional career but has been on a variety of NCATE boards and committees and could be of influence for your institution's accreditation under NCATE's collegiate standards. Which would you hire?" It was Dr. Dunn's opinion that many higher education institutions would go with the person who had the knowledge of the standards and could offer influence to the college's success.

As we will discuss in another chapter, about curriculum, the perfect school, beyond focusing on standards, would give ample opportunity for creativity in the curricular content while allowing further creativity in the instructional process. From our standpoint, it would be incredibly irresponsible not to hire a Nobel Prize winner, both for the dollars and prestige it would bring to the institution and for the opportunity it would bring the students and staff to spend time with a great thinker.

Fellow author Max McGee relates an example of this need. He took a class in graduate school at the University of Chicago from James Coleman, author of *The Coleman Report*.[2] The class was in

---

[1] *A Nation at Risk,* U.S. Government Publications, April, 1983.
[2] Coleman, J. and E. Campbell, C. Hobson, J. McPartland, A. Mood, F.D. Weinfeld, and R. York. *Equality of Educational Opportunity* (The Coleman Report). Washington D.C.: Department of Health, Education, and Welfare,1966.

mathematical sociology. Max relates how much more he learned beyond the topic through the class discussions and conversations about Coleman's dedication to students, about the plight of poverty kids, and how they were disenfranchised by the educational system. He also learned how good research could drive the national educational agenda and how the power of one person could truly make a difference.

The third recommendation provided by *A Nation at Risk* was that more time be devoted to the learning of these newly established, more rigorous standards. Some of these recommendations have been implemented, some not. For example, the commission recommended more home work. This seems to have been enacted in many schools and classrooms throughout the country.. The commission also recommended extending school days to seven hours and expanding the school year from the current length to a school year of over 200 days. The authors of this book supported this concept in their earlier book, ***What Every Superintendent and Principal Needs to Know,*** but it has not come to fruition. We hope that the longer school day and longer school year will take place in the future. A perfect school would be more attuned to parental and societal needs as it better prepares students to be successful citizens. This would include more school days than the current agrarian nine-month system adopted in the 1900s to accommodate a rural society. A perfect school needs a longer school day and a longer school year, in part to give schools the opportunity to restore neglected segments of the curriculum like programs in vocational training, fine/practical arts, and physical development. Enrichment programs about character development, cultural diversity, positive mental attitude, and violence prevention could then be added while still maintaining high standards in reading and math. A longer school year would help lessen the loss of knowledge that students experience during the summer months when no instruction takes place.

The fourth series of recommendations of *A Nation at Risk* dealt with making teaching a "more rewarding and respected profession." Many of these suggestions have not led to action. For example, while salaries have increased, they are still not professionally competitive, market sensitive, and performance based as stated in *A Nation at Risk.*.

It will be difficult to give teachers a performance-based salary as described in the report because kids are not widgets—each individual has unique needs. In addition, some students come from highly supportive parental situations, while others have virtually no support at home. Consequently, from a merit standpoint, it's virtually impossible to compare teachers who have a vast majority of students with little support with teachers who have students with substantial support. To establish that fair rewards take place, adjustments also must be made for the different environments in which teachers work. Other status aspects of the report that simply have not taken place include an 11-month contract for teachers, so that both teaching and professional development can happen. That's hampered by the fact that in many states budget-line items have been eliminated in which professional development monies were extended to the local school district.

The fifth recommendation in *A Nation at Risk* dealt with leadership and fiscal support. The report says that state and local officials have the primary responsibility for financing and governing the schools. As we will discuss later in the chapter about finances, it is clearly evident that the federal government is giving state and local governments the primary responsibility for financing the schools, as is indicated by the lack of funds it has provided for federally-mandated special education programs under IDEA (Individual with Disabilities Education Act) and the No Child Left Behind Act. Paradoxically, this same No Child Left Behind Act has made a majority of state and local officials feel that the federal government is making every effort to govern the schools—so let's discuss this in a moment. Also, the commission said that the federal government should help meet the additional needs of groups of students such as the gifted and talented, the socio-economically disadvantaged, minority and language minority students, and the handicapped. But the federal government has failed miserably in its effort to aid those groups. A perfect school needs all the proposals of the *A Nation at Risk* report implemented and adequately financed.

As we look at this report, one would conclude that the American educational system is in total disarray. Yet this is not the opinion shared worldwide. For example, in 2003 I had an opportunity to speak with an exceptional student named Eping from Singapore, which, according to test results, is educationally the leading nation in the world. Eping expressed my own feelings when he said, "We in Singapore do not understand the constant complaints about American education. We know that if we are going to develop higher order thinking skills, we have to come to the United States to further our learning."

Eping's example tells us that educational systems in the United States must be doing something right. Instead of celebrating our successes in education, our society is placing blame on the educational system for its societal problems. *A Nation at Risk* was quite willing to blame education for the poor economy of the early 1980s though, ironically, that same educational system was not celebrated in the 1990s when the economy was at its highest peace-time level ever.

One of the major long-term federal impacts on education occurred when Congress passed IDEA (Individuals with Disabilities Education Act) in 1975. This law had the laudable goal of providing equal opportunities for all children, including those children who have special academic, physical, social, and emotional needs. As this book is printed, more than six million students with a variety of special needs are served throughout the United States.[3]

IDEA demonstrates again that the devil is in the details. The original concept of this law was good because it caused educators throughout this nation to look at ways of helping students with disabilities. The four purposes of PL-142 (IDEA) include:

- to assure that all children with disabilities have available to them…a free appropriate public education which emphasizes special education and related services designed to meet their unique needs

- to assure that the rights of children with disabilities and their parents…are protected

- to assist states and localities to provide for the education of all children with disabilities

- to assess and assure the effectiveness of efforts to educate all children with disabilities[4]

The major problem with this legislation has been its funding. The law included a provision that the federal government would pay for 40% of the average per-student cost with special needs. To

---

[3] See www.nationaleducationassociation.com..

[4] *Education for All Handicapped Children's Act of 1975.*

quote the National Education Association website, "The federal government in 2004 is providing local school districts fewer than 20% of its financial commitment rather than the 40% commitment originally promised by the law, creating a shortfall for state and local school districts. This shortfall creates a burden on local communities and denies full opportunity to all students—with and without disabilities." To create a perfect school, the obvious—and actual—inequity would have to be corrected. Both regular and special education students alike are being held back from their potential success because of the financial deprivation created at the federal level.

For a perfect school, if funding of the 40% existed, a sufficient number of classrooms could become available, as would adequate time for teachers and therapists to discuss individual student needs while planning appropriate activities. It would also provide the parents easy-to-read parent rights forms and easy access to support personnel at the school. The Individualized Education Plan is designed for the student by therapists, teachers, and parents in such a way that educational goals are challenging yet achievable. Assessments are fair and provide information that leads to instructional improvement without demoralizing the student. Positive mental attitude programs are set up to enhance the self- esteem of special needs students.

No Child Left Behind Act

In 2002, President George W. Bush signed Federal legislation entitled the No Child Left Behind Act. Many feel this law has had the greatest federal impact on local education entities since the passage of IDEA in 1975. It looked wonderful on paper and had bi-partisan support in Congress. Some of its goals included more funding to schools, lowering of the achievement gap, higher graduation rates, students being taught by highly qualified teachers, higher attendance rates, and students taught in a safe environment with more local control. Another laudable premise behind the law is that all schools should be held accountable for the success of their students and should constantly strive for academic improvement.

The problem is that much of the determination whether or not a school and/or district is successful is based upon the results of a single achievement test developed in each state, presuming that the quality and complexity of teaching and learning can be adequately and solely assessed that way. Yet anybody associated with education knows that one test cannot adequately determine student success.

Most states have had testing programs in place since the mid 1980s. Our research has found that the vast majority of the districts that had low test scores in the 1980s still have low test scores now. This further supports the premise that while assessment is important, it is not the only important aspect of student learning.

The perfect school would have good instruction, parental support, students who are taught self-discipline, and the availability of positive peers. The perfect school would also teach healthy lifestyles, provide a well-rounded and quality curriculum, and receive adequate financial support from federal, state, and local sources. This money would in turn be spent in a student-centered way that would give students the ability to develop their future career strengths.

Students can learn, but they learn at different rates and their learning can be negatively impacted by issues such as poverty, mobility, divorce, and environmental problems that divert their major focus from learning. Also, if they lack the basic needs like food, shelter, clothing, and safety, they will not maximize their efforts in reading, writing, and arithmetic. All of these components are related to parenting and the student's life at home. Parents continue to be a major force behind educational success. Along with the educational standards set by the local community, the support by parents of the school system is the greatest component to a successful school district. This particularly includes the local community, which must demand quality schools. If the community and parents demand quality education, support the professional educators, and insist upon high student achievement, the result will be student success.

Let's also discuss some detail devils that have not been considered in this legislation. Most Americans believe that a child's test scores only count one time. This has not turned out to be true under the No Child Left Behind Act. One child's score can count up to five times each in reading and math test results. For instance, a Hispanic child from a low income family who is in a Special Education Program could be scored in the following sub-groups: (1) All Students, (2) Hispanic Sub-group, (3) Low Income Sub-group, (4) Special Education Sub-group, and (5) Limited English Proficient Sub-group. Now let's say that the child does not meet state standards. This one child will count against the school's results ten different times, five times in the reading results and five times in the math results. If the school does not meet state standards in any one of those ten categories, the school will be sanctioned. "Sanctioned" basically says that if a school does not meet state standards in any sub-group or other identified category such as attendance or graduation rates, the school will have to offer options such as school choice and supplemental educational services, like support training through agencies such as the Sylvan Learning Center. Eventually, if it continues to fall short of state standards, the district might be reorganized, with the Board of Directors and possibly the superintendent dismissed under the current NCLB guidelines. Many schools that are considered to be the very best and have been recognized for academic excellence have been sanctioned under the law's requirements.

Are there answers to this dilemma, given that all schools want to improve and need to know how many and which students are not meeting state standards? Yes. Have realistic, researched goals based upon a framework of objectives that schools can strive for and have a chance of achieving, within their environment.

Assessments are definitely part of this solution, particularly if used in ways that are student centered. We must face the realization that all students will not focus their success in the areas of reading and math, thus we must use the education system to identify each individual's strengths and weaknesses. If we do this, we can change the perception of American education and further help students improve.

Let's look at school vouchers. Many elected officials feel that if a school does not meet state standards over a period of time, its students should be given tuition vouchers of up to $1,500 to attend a private or parochial schools. This sounds like a good idea, but the details say otherwise. First, many private and parochial school educators have quietly stated to this author that if they were given a $1,500 voucher they would raise tuition an additional $1,500. Second, these same educators told me that they want to control which students enroll in their schools. They do not want to deal with some of the problematic situations that have been thrust upon the public school sector. And third, private and parochial school educators have stated to me that they do not want to be under the government's system of rules for education since they feel that many of these rules stifle potential academic success.

One of the fundamental components of the No Child Left Behind Act is the concept of school choice whereby the parent has the opportunity to choose the school they want their child to attend. Again, this sounds better than it is in fact. I have been interested in school choice for years; my dissertation was written about school choice. Here is what my research found.

1. Parents who have particular interest in their child's education use schools as a criterion for choosing where they live. As such, parents are already using school choice in America. Parents do not need governmental rules to insinuate that they are not smart enough or care enough to determine where their child attends school. And when parents don't care, a government rule is not going to help the situation. We need to look at the parenting taking place and other ways that the government and the school can provide family intervention for the benefit of the child.

2. If school choice were implemented, parents overwhelmingly indicated they would keep their students in the school they presently attend.

3. When parents used school choice before the No Child Left Behind Act was implemented, it was many times for reasons other than academic. For example, if their child's caregiver was in another school's boundaries, then school choice took place. Similar choice selections were used to facilitate athletic and fine arts desires.

4. Transporting students from one school to another is a huge logistical and financial problem for both parents and school districts. Many times, instructional time is lost because of the need to meet transportation requirements.

5. A majority of parents want greater financial and academic support for the school their child presently attends.

School choice currently exists. School competition is already here. Some would say that those that do not fully support school choice are trying to skirt competition. Parents are now looking at test scores more and more to choose where they live. Personally, I would welcome school choice if the previously stated issues are addressed and the rules are the same for all schools—public, private, and parochial schools alike. Competitors for public dollars must accept all children despite their disabilities, maintain children who are experiencing discipline problems, accept children of all economic levels, maintain school safety requirements, comply with the same paperwork requirements, and report yearly test scores of every student, including home-schooled students.

The question becomes how can a perfect school survive under this environment? How can we take this law that started out with such high expectations and mold it into a usable document for school and student improvement? The perfect school would seek higher test scores, school accountability, a faculty of highly qualified teachers, optimal attendance and graduation rates, and students being taught in a safe environment. A perfect school would support the continuation of the basic premises of the No Child Left Behind Act but would demand common sense changes in the current legislation and rules. But to reach that perfection it would need these modifications:

1. Limit the sanctions to the bottom 10% of the schools in each state so that intervention can efficiently support those schools both academically and financially.

2. Tweak the assessment measures of the sub-groups for "special education" and "limited English proficient" so it is possible for the students to meet state standards using adaptations in the assessments. In special education, for example, there is a sub-group of students that cannot meet state standards to get into the program under the Federal IDEA legislation, yet this same sub-group is expected to meet state standards under the Federal No Child Left Behind Act. The two laws contradict each other. They need to be made congruent. Special education students should be assessed, but at their current identified level of achievement. Children with disabilities would have their assessment plans dictated by the IEP (Individualized Edu-

cation Plan). LEP (Limited English Proficient) students should be assessed within their appropriate programs so that their test results can give an indication of student success.

3. Encourage extensive research to see what a good benchmark for student progress is. For example, all researchers in the field of education know that it is impossible for 100% of the students to reach state standards. What is an achievable goal? This should be established so that schools have a number to strive for that makes teaching the standards doable. To personalize this issue, I am 56 years old and weigh 230 pounds. If I was told I had to jump over a six-foot bar by this time next year or be fined $1,000, I would ask a couple of quick questions. One, can I use a trampoline or some other source to help me get over the bar? Two, can I get some individuals who are very strong to throw me over the bar? If the answer to these questions is no, I will simply write the check for $1,000 because I know that the goal is not achievable. This is where we are with the current 100% goal. It is unachievable. Are diminishing test results inevitable because schools, realizing they cannot meet the required goal, won't put as much effort into the learning process as they could?

4. While the No Child Left Behind Act causes states to focus monies on the improvement of reading and math, attention must be paid that this isn't done at the expense of gifted, fine/practical arts, physical development, vocational programs, violence prevention, and character development programs.

Many questions still linger in our schools. Will there be adequate funding? Will we truly start analyzing the impact of poverty and alcohol and other drugs on student success? Will states take the initiative to assume control of schools that are not having academic success? Will we establish achievable goals? Will professional development funds be made available for the improvement of instruction?

We have so many opportunities under the No Child Left Behind Act and there are many good things going on in schools because of the Act. For example, for an assignment in my graduate curriculum class at McKendree College, I asked my students to reflect on the No Child Left Behind Act. One of my students, Jennifer Relleke, gave an interesting and positive perspective. She stated:

> Most people I have encountered in the education community seem to use NCLB as if speaking a dirty word. It requires "change"—another dirty word. It has too many rules to decipher. It is something to "get around." It labels schools that do not meet its unrealistic expectations. It uses threats to coerce schools into implementation. It has taken essentially three days of standardized tests to a whole new level of exaggerated importance.
>
> That being said, it has been through my reflection on NCLB that I have found all of the positive growth that NCLB has brought to our school.
>
> When I began my teaching career, focusing on school improvement was an activity that involved constructing a plan—and the curriculum was the textbook. Ten years and many grants later, life in our district is very different. I have seen many wonderful changes in my school. When asked to reflect, I find it has to be in large part to NCLB. Three of the areas my school has improved in is data analysis, school leadership, and curriculum planning.
>
> NCLB has forced our staff to begin collecting data from a variety of sources. The analysis of that data is beneficial to our students in countless ways. Knowing more about your students and their lives guides the decisions that affect their educational and emotional growth.
>
> As a part of a Comprehensive School Reform grant, our school created leadership teams. Those teams have involved teachers in the decision-making process. Participation on a leadership committee helped to make me aware of a variety of sound educational practices that were not being widely used in my building. It also facilitated cooperation between other middle schools. In our district replacing a competitive relationship with a cooperative one has been beneficial for schools. Making school reform a more grassroots type of movement has made it more effective.

Most importantly, our district has had to increase its awareness of our curriculum and our state's standards, and effective teaching practices. The state test has such high stakes that it has forced us to become cognizant of the state's expectations. Focusing on the state's standards is becoming a way of life. Using the assessment framework, we are making strides in the alignment of our curriculum in all areas. We are continually receiving in-service on effective teaching practices. We still have much to do to meet the changing needs of our students, but efforts are being made to improve academics at our school.

My conclusion comes as a surprise to me, but my reflection upon NCLB has found it to be a worthwhile piece of legislation. I know that I am a better teacher because my district was forced to try to meet its standards. It is also much in need of reform. As long as NCLB's goals are unattainable, it will continue to be a dirty word.

Achieving "perfection" is too utopian to suggest as the cause of the four bills and reports cited in this chapter; still, each at its core seeks just that, the perfect school. Positive steps are being taken because of the letter and spirit of such legislation, yet their wording and actual implementation are hurdles we must resolve to even approach that perfection. The best places to start are with accountability, a challenging curriculum, and better teaching practices.

"Success hinges on a passion for excellence."

John F. Kennedy (1917-63)

Chapter Ten

Gathering Data to Help Improve Student Success

Jim Rosborg

The perfect school (1) works to gather data to help student's improve, (2) develops instructional strategies through a collaborative process, (3) constantly re-evaluates the strength of the instructional plan and student learning, (4) implements positive approaches to data communication, and (5) deals with proper classroom assessment procedures to use data for student improvement.

This chapter will discuss the importance of gathering data and using those results for school improvement. A perfect school works to develop and apply a consistent philosophy about student evaluation. We wish to encourage you to develop your own school-wide diagnostic procedures based upon an aligned curriculum and the use of obtained data.

Needless to say, how a school and staff uses, analyzes, and implements the results of assessment and its ensuing data is of critical importance. Many schools do not take that critical step forward simply because they do not spend enough time going over their data and developing implementation strategies that can help students improve.

The first thing that a perfect school understands is that teachers have to be part of the analysis of the data and the decision-making process. If a district truly wants the decisions made in the planning process to be executed, teachers have to be engaged in the process. Implementation takes commitment. Many districts make the mistake of not understanding the need to include teachers in the data analysis process from start to finish. The districts that do not understand the importance of this concept simply do not get the commitment from their staff. Consequently, successful implementation does not take place.

In gathering data, the successful curriculum leader realizes that not all teachers want to be involved in the initial data collection, although they do want to be involved in the decision-making process. What do you do? Focus on those teachers who want to be involved in the initial data collection and assessment and pay them to help analyze the data. Then bring in the rest of the staff to fine-tune the recommendations for improvement so that all staff members will have ownership in the school improvement process.

Once the perfect school understands the key participants and the procedures for successful improvement strategy implementation, then hard data developed through the efforts of the initial data analysis team has to be used to make decisions. This can include local assessments, staff surveys, student surveys, parent surveys, community surveys, state tests, national tests, and any other data deemed necessary for students to improve. Administrators can also analyze the data and give input to the data results that will be submitted to the staff. Once the data assessment team has established the data they are going use, certain things have to happen.

1. The total school team needs to identify strengths in the curriculum. There also needs to be an effort to celebrate the strengths, build upon them, and communicate those strengths to staff members, parents, and other key stakeholders. Initially, some staff members are hesitant to "brag" about their success. After a few times of implementing this success strategy, those fears generally subside. For example, state test data showed that in my district Belleville #118 was scoring significantly higher in writing and math problem solving. The district had made these areas a focus of our professional development activities. We celebrated the success of our efforts and sent teachers to other districts in the area to help their staff improve. These successes were based upon sound data known by surrounding schools. Our efforts to work with these schools helped elevate our overall perception in the

area. It also brought the district positive press releases which further enhanced the community's feelings about the district.

2. In a perfect school the team needs to identify instructional weaknesses where problems exist. Those problem areas should be stated in terms of the hard data obtained from tests and surveys. A clear example of this was shared by co-author Max McGee. The staff in his district in Wilmette, Illinois, discovered that their male students were getting lower grades and also scoring lower in state and national tests than the girls in reading and language arts. They broke down the specific data to show the gender inequity. Rather than just blaming the boys for being lazy, through professional staff efforts the teachers changed their approach to teaching the male students. The male scores went up—and so did the female scores! Hard data lead to those improvements.

3. A perfect school must remember to focus the improvements in select, identified areas. The initial data collection team can break down the areas of improvement into ten specific categories for instructional improvement, and the total faculty can then reduce those to five. The areas must be specific to the objective. For example, in the area of mathematics a school can't say that it is good in computation but needs to improve in algebra and problem solving. Each is a distinct course. The staff has to determine which specific areas of algebra or which specific problem solving techniques need instructional focus. The team should also look at the demographics of their school district and devise an action plan to individualize the student's academic needs. Trends must also be studied to see what instructional strategies should be implemented. By knowing the students in the district, a school must define the particular areas it thinks need improvement to implement its instructional plan.

4. Once instructional strategies have been developed, the team then needs to develop an evaluation system to determine how effective the remedial instructional strategies have been. The test to evaluate the success of these in-

structional strategies should be developed during this same in-service. Timelines should be established when this evaluation will take place. Instructional time emphasis allocations should also be discussed. How much instructional time will be devoted to the identified improvement standards? How many times will the concept be reviewed? When will the evaluation of students take place regarding these specific concepts? What additional follow-ups will be needed once this evaluation has taken place? How does the school transition to focus instructional strategies on other academic problem areas once improvement has taken place in the initially identified problem areas? When does it stop evaluating? Never. Some instructional improvement will always be needed. Balance is vital. Neither too many areas of improvement nor too few. Improvement is a constant work in progress.

5. At the conclusion of the strategies in 1-4, the team might discuss such issues as discipline, safety, respect, self-esteem, character development, etc. A general brainstorming session should take place regarding to the team's observations in the areas of teaching and learning, student progress, and the environment of the school as a whole. Instead of a gripe session, this is a problem-solving opportunity to improve both academics and the entire school environment. A good brainstorming session would follow agreed upon parameters and be positive in its goals and outcomes.

For perfect schools there is a caution to note. Often schools and districts make the analysis of data too complicated. They infuse too many statistical variables for the average teacher to understand. A school district can have eye-popping charts and graphs but if the key stakeholders don't understand their implications, they are valueless.

Public Relations and Reporting Scores

A perfect school will focus on how to effectively communicate state test results to parents and the community. If we agree that 100% of the students will not meet or exceed state goals, how does the perfect, or any, school explain that it is doing well even though it has been sanctioned under the guidelines of the No Child Left Behind Act? This is an uncomfortable arena. A public relations program that accentuates the positive aspects of the school will help. These are areas where good public relations can be of assistance:

- Collect and share positive perceptions of the school, particularly those areas identified by parents who have children attending the school.

- Send out questionnaires to teachers, parents, students, and community members as to how they feel the school is doing. These responses can lead to school improvement if handled in a professional way.

- Circulate encouraging newsletters to the parents, community, and other key stakeholders. Don't forget senior citizens; they are a major component to the success of any election initiative. In the newsletter, report where instructional improvement has taken place, areas where you have met or exceeded state goals, how you compare with districts of similar demographics, successful areas outside of the testing program, the district's positive working environment, the support you get from parents, awards the school has achieved, your curriculum, and other changes that are taking place.

- Celebrate your diversity, but explain how a diverse school setting leads to having more scoring categories under the NCLB, which in turn leads to a greater chance of being sanctioned. Develop charts showing the progress of all subgroups that reside in your school.

- Set up a town hall meeting: a NCLB Tutorial. Educate the public.

- Focus on the areas where the school had particular academic success. This can be enhanced by involving parent/community members from different NCLB sub-groups to explain what positive changes have affected their child.

- Focus on parental involvement in the school. Where appropriate, tie this parental involvement into positive student performance.

- Discuss the strategies the school is pursuing to achieve academic improvement. Explain the school's action plan.

- Tell how the development program has been organized.

- Point out growth specific to the sanctioned groups, and how they are the positive results of programs that are currently in place.

- Educate related government leaders about the school's specific need to facilitate improvement.

- Show genuine concern for the areas where you are not meeting state standards. Emphasis that *all* kids are important to your school and that the school is striving to make all of them successful citizens using each of the student's respective strengths as platforms for success.

- Invite the media to come to your school to observe its positive academic environment.

Policy of Student Assessment
in the Classroom

Another important component of gathering hard data takes place in the classroom itself. This is where the collaboration team needs to be involved. The perfect school has an established and consistent diagnostic plan that is easily understood by students, parents, staff, and key stakeholders; student evaluation is an integral part of that total instructional process. The diagnostic plan helps ensure that teachers have a thorough and uniform understanding of all district-wide evaluation components. The diagnostic guide outlines the materials, instruments, and records that are vital to the identification of student progress, with the materials to maintain the data. This plan includes professional development activities that ensure consistency in the process. In this process, some specific questions of grading philosophy will certainly be discussed by the staff. These philosophies need to be molded together to have one reporting instrument that is easily understood by parents and other key stakeholders.

To check a perfect school's assessment effectiveness, ask these questions.

- Do teachers have ownership in your reporting instrument? Does the school report card effectively communicate to parents?

- What kind of communication system do you have with parents?

- Are parents required to come to meet directly with the teacher at conference time? Is there follow-up with the parents who don't show up for the conference?

- Is there an alignment of local, state, and national tests with the instructional program so that evaluation and improvement can take place?

- Does the school use data to help formulate needs for staff improvement? Does it have strong local assessments that are included in the data collection?

- Can the district improve in the variety of assessments used for grading student achievement?

- What additional strategies can administration and staff use to help students take greater responsibility for their learning?

Summary

Most individuals when discussing the reporting of student success in the classroom simply refer to the report card. As we have seen in this chapter, there is much more than the school report card to show how a student is doing. We should gather as much hard data as we can when discussing students. This should include national, state, and local tests. It can also include assessments of homework, student effort, and attitude. Helping students to improve is a complex scenario that takes collaboration and commitment by all professionals.

Chapter Eleven

Bridging the Academic Gap

Max McGee and Jim Rosborg

> The perfect school makes it a top priority to (1) identify gaps in achievement among racial and ethnic groups, between students from low-income families and their peers, and between boys and girls; (2) craft a culture of high expectations for achievement, behavior, and success for every child; (3) make literacy the top academic priority; (4) reach out to parents and caregivers; (5) extend the school day and/or year, and (6) assure that all teachers are highly skilled and committed to the school's mission.

Identifying Gaps

In the past few years, the "Achievement Gap" has become part of the common vernacular. With the high profile of the NCLB, it has become even more definitively documented that minority children from economically low-income families generally do not do nearly as well in reading, writing, and mathematics as their white and Asian classmates or their peers from middle class and affluent families.

The proof of enormous gaps in reading and mathematics is in the numbers. Using the statistics from Illinois where the school population of 2.2 million children includes more than 850,000 low-income families, the most recent 2005 data indicates that the gaps exist at the beginning, middle, and end of a student's education.

In third grade, the gap between students from low-income families and their peers was 32 percentage points in reading and

36 percentage points in mathematics. Specifically, only 48% of low-income third grade students met state reading standards and 64% met state math standards. These figures compare to their more affluent peers who had 80% meet state reading standards and 90% meet state math standards.

The gaps at eighth grade and eleventh grade are significant too. The gap in eighth grade reading is 23 points and there is a 36-point gap in mathematics. The gaps in eleventh grade are 30 and 36 percentage points respectively for reading and math, with just one in four poor students able to attain state math standards.

Moreover, because more African American students and Hispanic students live in low-income families, the achievement gap is stratified by race. In 2005, approximately 78% of white students and 84% of Asian students met or exceeded state reading standards compared to 41% of African American students and 56% of Hispanic students.

In eighth grade, 82% of white students and 87% of Asian students met or exceeded state reading standards while 53% of African American and 60% of Hispanic students met or exceeded standards. Eighth grade writing scores show an even larger gap. On the 2004 state writing assessment (it was not administered in 2005), approximately 75% of Asian students and 68% of white students met or exceeded state standards compared to 33% and 37% of their African American and Hispanic peers.

By eleventh grade an enormous gap in reading achievement exists between white and minority students and between poor students and their peers. As a result, graduating high school students who are stratified by race and income:

- In 2005, 63% of low-income students did not meet state standards in eleventh grade, but 67% of non-poor students did meet or exceed state standards.
- In 2005, fewer than 40% of minority students met state reading standards, while more than 67% of white students met or exceeded state reading standards.
- Moreover, the gaps between racial groups and between the poor and non-poor high school students are scarcely closing. In the last four years, the achievement gap between white and African American students and between poor and non-poor students only decreased by one point!

In more homogeneous schools gaps also exist. Recent articles in the popular press—"The Trouble with Boys," in *Newsweek*[1] and "Boys and Books: Boy Trouble" in the *New Republic Online*[2]— have drawn attention to the fact that boys lag far behind girls in reading and writing across all ethnic groups, all racial ethnic groups, and all grade levels. For example, according to the 2005 Illinois state test results, the gap in reading among all boys and girls in eleventh grade in 2005 is statistically significant. While 63% of the girls met or exceeded state standards, just 55.9% of the boys did. The situation with writing is worse. The last time Illinois gave a writing assessment, in 2004, eleventh grade girls outscored boys by a statistically significant margin of more than 10%! Approximately 65.3% of the girls met or exceeded state standards compared to 53.7% of the boys.

In the perfect school the principal and teachers work together to identify gaps. They examine the results of state test scores and local assessments. They analyze grades to see if a regular pattern exists and they survey parents and teachers. They also examine other data sources such as placement in special education services or reading or math support. They look for patterns in placement in classes for the gifted and talented as well as in school disciplinary records. One school we know even examined library records and found that girls checked out books far more frequently, and that the books boys checked out were more limited in topic and genre.

When the perfect school finds gaps, they act upon Jim Collins' advice to "confront the brutal facts."[3] In the typical school data, showing gaps is often explained away or even ignored. We have heard teachers and principals actually blame gaps on the quality of the state test or even worse on the parents or the students themselves. "Boys will never read or write as well as girls. They are just not wired that way," noted one clueless educator. In the perfect school, however, the identification of a gap is a clarion call to action, "To arms, to arms—a segment of our students is not progressing." Leaders in the perfect school create a sense of urgency and even outrage.

---

[1] Peg Tyre, January 30, 2006.

[2] Richard Whitmire, January 18, 2006.

[3] Collins, J., ***Good to Great: Why Some Companies Make the Leap and Others Don't***.

Crafting a Culture

While the pernicious achievement gap continues to be the Public Enemy Number One of education (if not America), perfect schools around the country have proven what authors Robert Barr and William Parrett and what Katie Haycock and her colleagues from Education Trust have shown with numerous examples: "a good school can overcome the debilitating effects of poverty and a dysfunctional family."[4] Barr makes it very clear that schools fail poor/minority students when they:

- Hold low expectations for achievement
- Assign students to inexperienced teachers
- Fail to teach reading and basic skills
- Retain, track, and improperly assign students to special education
- Blame students' families
- Employ a bell curve mentality

On the flip side, schools that have a culture of success are distinguished by:

- An exceptional leader who stirs everyone to action
- A collective commitment to closing the gaps
- A pervasive sense of efficacy (we are responsible for closing gaps and we can close gaps)
- Every staff member sharing high expectations for every student
- Professional development for the collective, not individual, good

We have seen perfect schools in action and know they are different almost from the moment we walk in the door. The mission is usually sensed when one enters the building, though it cannot be immediately seen. Even a brief conversation with any staff member shows that all feel an intense responsibility for the academic success and emotional growth of every child in the building.

---

[4] Barr, Robert, "Closing the Achievement Gap: Every Day, Every Student a Success." Presentation to the No Child Left Behind Conference, Chicago, Illinois, January 15, 2007.

Another characteristic of the culture of perfect schools is the close bond among the teachers. "We are a family," "our people genuinely care about each other," and "this is our house" are representative comments reflecting the tightly shared beliefs and support network that brings together the entire building—principal, teachers, aides, secretaries, custodians, etc. In these schools, cooperation and communication flourish. Though occasional disagreements erupt, by and large they are families who have internal support and enjoy and are proud of each other. A key piece of this culture is where students fit. The children are not "little people," "blank slates," or "empty buckets." They, too, are part of the family, and the culture of perfect schools includes them. The staff believes in the importance of knowing the whole child and working with his or her family. As one teacher noted, "We have to know where the child lives."

One other common characteristic of a perfect school staff is the work ethic. Closing gaps is extraordinarily demanding, especially the gap between low-income students and their peers. Unlike schools serving wealthier students, one doesn't just start the day teaching knowing the kids will be ready to learn. First things first. Said one principal, "The kids live in pain; they have garbage heaped on them, so school must be safe and supportive." Every principal and every teacher, if asked, could share a story of the challenges children face as a matter of course.

Neighborhoods aren't always safe places, but the home can sometimes be even more dangerous. Family trauma, hunger, toothaches become a part of daily life. The successful schools are those that work hard to assure nutrition, safety, and security *before* teaching. The school day for these teachers begins well before 9 a.m. and lasts well past 3 p.m. More than a few recounted parent conferences in students' homes, in getting to school at 7 a.m. and staying well past 7 p.m. to work with parents or with students or plan with other teachers or prepare for the challenges of the next day. Principals and teachers told of their long hours, their home visits, the out-of-pocket money they spent on materials, and the like. These stories were neither complaints nor boasts, just descriptions of what it takes to help poor kids learn. Simply put, the perfect school's culture is one of hard work.

A culture of success also includes helping children realize their responsibility to others and providing the education, direction, and guidance to help them become good parents and responsible citizens. The perfect school demonstrates its belief that all kids, regardless of their ethnicity or financial conditions, have the capacity to be good kids. Rather than focusing on the small percentage of students who consistently do not follow the rules, the focus must be on celebrating those students who are good school citizens. Otherwise, it adversely affects the school's ability to help all students improve academically.

The culture of the school doesn't just happen. It is planted, grown, and nurtured. The key figure is the principal or a staff leader. An earlier chapter went into detail about the "perfect principal," but here is a brief taste of what we have observed.

They are clearly leaders of learning—for both staff and students. They combine a big vision with the ability to manage day-to-day operations. The principals work hard at being visible. There are incredible demands on their time, but there is always time for a walk through. They believe that the kids have to know them as people and not as the figurehead of the school.

In the perfect school the principals think strategically. They are well read and current, and they are perceived as knowledgeable. Staff meetings are mini-workshops, a chance to be professionals. They understand the demands of working with low-income students and ensure that behavior does not get in the way of learning.

The principals are resourceful. In lean financial times they strive to preserve proven programs at all costs. They understand and "walk the talk" of hiring and keeping good people. In addition to aggressively pursuing grants to fund programs and practices, they stick with them long after the funding expires.

The principals lead by example. They share a remarkable work ethic and have positive relationships with staff and students. "We work hard but we have fun," commented one teacher. The principals have earned a reputation for doing "whatever it takes" to help students, including conducting house calls with teachers. The teachers rely on them to set the tone with parents. They are collegial and respectful of staff and students. They focus on results and have high expectations. They help teachers deal with state mandates and model the belief that every child can succeed. Young or old, thin or not, they exude high energy. They are aggressive about getting books and recognize and commend excellence. Empathy for the teachers' task is evident, but several also remarked about how their "no excuses" policy is accepted by their unions. They encourage innovation and they have the courage to take on the bad teachers. Many are model teachers themselves. Some have spent many years in the classroom, some were former Title I teachers, and some were former special education teachers. In any case, almost all school leaders make it a practice of doing some teaching or other demonstration work.

Leadership in the perfect schools is a shared commitment. Teacher leadership is encouraged. Teachers are given time to work together within their school and across their district. At one particularly successful school, the teachers lead the staff meetings. These, as well as staff meetings in most high-poverty, high-performing schools, are more like mini-workshops on instruction or assessment. Everyone pulls together. One teacher we observed remarked, "Our principal gets buy-in. She makes the school warm and inviting for all." Another told us that her school's culture is "can do/will do."

The principal's direct involvement in the teaching and learning process is critical. As one teacher told SBE, "our staff is very involved in continuous improvement. We work together in teams and make instructional decisions together. We all share the responsibility for continuous improvement ... our staff is very familiar with our school goals and our school improvement plan. Adjustments are made to our structure based on assessment results." Says another of her principal, "The principal constantly monitors classrooms and student progress. If she finds deficiencies, she looks to find the causes and then makes changes to eliminate them—even moving teachers from grade to grade, if necessary. She does an informal performance check frequently and makes sure horizontal and vertical articulation occurs."

Principals in perfect schools understand the importance of closing the gaps, as well as the pain. They encourage and expect risk-taking and support their teachers' innovative ideas, even if they don't always work. The sense of urgency is always present.

A Hispanic principal of one of our perfect schools continually reminds teachers, parents, and the greater community that the time for action is now, quoting Gabriela Mistral, the former poet laureate of Chile.[5]

---

[5] Mistral. Gabriela, "Su Nombre es Hoy," *Gabriela Mistral Selected Poems*. Burns, P. and S. Ortiz-Carboneres, translators. Oxford, UK: Aris and Phillips, 2006.

Somos culpables de muchos errores y muchos defectos,
Pero nuestro peor crimen es el abandonamiento de los niños,
Descuidando la fuente de la vida.
Muchos de las cosas que necesitamos pueden esperar.
El niño no ...
A ella no podemos contestarle "Mañana."
Su nombre es "Hoy."

We are guilty of many errors and many faults,
But our worst crime is abandoning the children,
Neglecting the fountain of life.
Many of the things we need can wait.
Not the child ...
To her we cannot answer "Tomorrow."
Her name is "Today."

Literacy is the Top Priority

Bridging the gap doesn't happen unless all children learn to read
and write well. There are enough volumes about teaching reading
and writing to fill a library floor, so rather than repeat those findings, let's share a few examples of what we have seen in perfect
schools.

"Early literacy is a must," said one teacher. "Kids come to us
not knowing their first and last names, not knowing their shapes,
not knowing sounds. They have an impaired vocabulary and little
exposure to books or any print." Every perfect school emphasizes
early literacy and provides intervention for struggling readers. Although there is not a common, or even prevalent, reading series or
curriculum, there are strong program commonalities; notably,
reading instruction in these schools has a strong emphasis on
phonics, fluency, and vocabulary development along with comprehension.

Contrary to many schools, perfect school classrooms have extensive classroom library collections, even if the school library is
limited. Principals and teachers find ways to get books into the
classroom, and then into the homes. "Books in a Bag" was one
school's solution to be sure that parents read with students. They
literally sent home a book in a baggie every Friday! Another

school held "family dinners" once every two weeks where students and parents read together after dinner.

The perfect high schools have found ways to restore the confidence of weak readers and writers. They teach struggling readers by using colorful, high-action, often edgy materials that are of high interest to the students. They make reading come alive by reading to students and teaching them to read aloud with expression. With coaching, the content area teachers quickly acquire the expertise to help their students unravel more complicated text. They find boy books and often use single-gender classes or groups when discussing literature.

To close the writing gap, teachers in the perfect school require and reward journaling. They help students create a voice and celebrate the smallest victories. Boys' writing clubs, "underground papers," and student written and performed plays are other successful techniques we have seen.

The point is that reading and writing come first. They are quite literally not only the quickest way to close the gap but the most important tools for success in school and beyond.

Reach out to Parents and Caregivers

Students are actually in the school less than ten percent of their life during their PK-12 educational "careers." Clearly, the home has enormous influence on a student's life and it is imperative that the home and school work together to bridge gaps. This is exponentially more challenging in high-poverty schools, where often there is little communication that takes place between the home and school. In the perfect school principals and teachers do not use poverty as an excuse. Below are a few examples of outreach that worked well in schools we observed that have a wide range of economic and ethnic diversity.

The goal of the perfect school is to find a way to both communicate with all parents and get them involved with the school. We found that in poorer environments parents appreciated teachers and administrators visiting their homes to talk about school issues. That required certain protocols. In one school the principal first sent letters to the parents so they knew a visit was coming, to avoid unwanted surprises. The staff always visited in pairs and attempted to find a time when children and parents were home together. These visits worked well. They let the parents know that the school wanted to relate to them and work together for the success of their children.

In Dr. Rosborg's district, which was the top in Illinois for closing the achievement gap, staff also had open houses in every school the two nights before the start of each new school year. One method they used to increase attendance was to withhold the name of the child's homeroom teacher or their class schedule before the open house. Consequently, the students themselves encouraged their parents to attend—they wanted to know who their teacher was going to be when they walked thru the doors on the first day!

Another method was to make parent conferences mandatory. They encouraged the parents to attend by handing out the student's report card at the parent conferences, and made it a warm, welcoming experience by having the school exceptionally clean and shiny and having ample refreshments and treats available.

To bridge the gap between home and school they also paid additional attention to students who were more than a year behind academically. The teacher and the parent worked together to identify the academic problem(s) the student was having and to formulate strategies for that student's academic improvement. They stressed study skills, organizational development activities, use of the public library, summer academic programs, and other forms of academic reinforcement that can occur in the home. Discussions also took place regarding the need for summer school or attending after-school academic and enrichment programs. More than anything, these specially adapted individual improvement plans opened the communication link between the home and the school.

Other methods that Belleville #118 used to get the parents into the school on a non-threatening basis included having socials, with ice cream, cake, chili, hot dogs, and hamburgers as incentives. Food worked. Often it was provided for special math nights, reading nights, technology nights, and science nights. During those events parents became students, actively participating in activities that their children had experienced in their classes. These were presented in a non-threatening, often entertaining way and staff was careful to be sure that the parents would be successful in every participatory activity. The expenses for these evenings were modest. Parents felt welcome at the school, walked away with a sense of accomplishment, and over time became far more active partners in their children's education. In the process, new avenues of communication were opened with those parents. For many, the process helped remove the negative school experiences the parents had felt as students or with their other children at other schools.

Belleville also made the schools a community center for parents and key stakeholders in the district. They developed walking tracks for people to use, improved playground structures, and worked with local parks and recreation departments to offer basketball, baseball, softball, soccer, and volleyball at the school's facilities.

Extend the School Day and/or Year

Closing the gap requires the perfect school to find more time for teaching the lower-performing students. This is easier said than done as the length of the school day and abbreviated school year make it nearly impossible to wring out an extra minute. Perfect schools schedule activities as a team to maximize large daily blocks of uninterrupted time. They even strive to minimize transition time between classes and even between lessons. After-school activities are a critical component of many schools' success. Thousands of children in perfect schools participate in at least one after-school activity each week, and some participate on a daily basis. Whether joining a photography club or preparing for the ISAT, students have many opportunities to do something after school. In poor communities parents do not have the resources to promote after-school activities even when they were available. After-school learning time matters a great deal.

Also, the perfect school uses summer school to extend academic learning time for a high percentage of students. Participation for four to six weeks in summer school reading and/or mathematics classes is the norm. Summer school isn't just for academics, it also provides time for field trips, classes, and activities for enrichment and enhancement. These experiences and activities may be the norm for middle class families, but they aren't for children of poverty. Consequently, Franklin School assured that weekly swim lessons and visits to Meramec Caverns, the Science Center, Raging Rivers, and the ballpark were available to children by working with the Neighborhood Association. The staff understood that in real life these were as important as academic tutoring, computer instruction, and classes on problems solving—which were also offered.

Highly Skilled and Committed Teachers

Note that we do not say "highly qualified." Though we believe all teachers should be "highly qualified," teachers committed to closing the gap need a whole lot more than a current certificate. Teaching to close gaps requires knowledge, skills, and disposition as well as the ability to leap tall buildings, be more powerful than a locomotive, and be faster than a speeding bullet. Sorry, we got carried away, but the fact is that many teachers do not have the background knowledge or mindset to teach poor, minority children; embrace, accept and capitalize on boyness, and differentiate their instruction so that children are not learning the way they teach but they are teaching the way children learn.

It is abundantly clear that these teachers sincerely believe that all students could learn, and their behaviors reflect this belief. As a group they have a fierce pride in assuring that each child succeeds. More than one teacher said, "We are on a mission." They are not invested in children's success to protect their job or make the school "look good"; rather, they treat each child as their own—close relationships, mutual respect and admiration, and genuine fondness characterize their classrooms. Positive messages abound, whether in personal interactions or displays on the walls. Though extraordinarily compassionate, these teachers are not about to accept excuses for low achievement or lack of effort. Instead, they incorporate a significant range of strategies and use a vast array of resources to help each individual child.

Because teachers are the launching pad of student success, school districts and their leaders should provide an environment in which the teacher can maximize his or her potential to help students become successful citizens. This process is best achieved by using a team approach with teachers and collaborating with them on key decisions, particularly concerning school curriculum.

"Collaboration" is a frequently used term, but is seldom practiced outside the perfect school. Collaboration begins with the understanding and sincere belief that the whole, literally, is greater than the sum of its parts. Like the go cart kit I bought for my gear head son, the powerful engine, gleaming steering wheel, sturdy tie rods, and myriad nuts and bolts looked great on the garage floor, but nothing moved until they were assembled into one smooth operating machine. In the perfect school, teachers revere and respect their peers and share a common commitment to work together for the good of the school, not for their own advancement or recognition.

Collaborative activities in the perfect school begin with a goal that usually comes from data that identifies a clear gap. Before jumping into solutions, they collaborate on developing a mission or goal statement and agreeing on measures for success. Measures can be improvement in test scores, but when collaboration is clicking teachers are quick to identify many more key measures of success. For example, if there is a gap between boys' reading scores and girls' reading scores, one measure may be to close the test score gap. Extra measures of success might be to have boys more actively participate in class discussions, check out books from the classroom and school library, volunteer to work as reading buddies with students from lower grades, read independently at home, pursue a project based on something they read, write their own story and book, and more.

In the perfect school collaborative conversations don't just happen at formal faculty meetings or on workshop days. They are an almost daily occurrence and arise at lunch hour, before school, or during planning period. In elementary schools they even happen on the playground while supervising recess.

Once the mission, goals, and measures are set, collaboration ratchets up further as teachers begin trying innovative approaches and sharing what works and what does not. The perfect school looks, sounds, and feels more like a laboratory than a school as teachers work individually or in teams to test their hypotheses about closing the gap and bring in activities from "best practices" or research that they have acquired from conversation, reading, or observations outside their school. In the perfect school, study groups spring up around particular issues related to the goal or mission and these "teams" readily share their knowledge with others.

Professional development in perfect schools looks far different and, as the data indicates, is far more successful than in most schools. Perfect schools frequently have staff development activities that are delivered on site and are tied to the school improvement plan. Whether the professional development is about charac-

ter education, guided reading, technology applications, assessment, curriculum, recent research, or structured routines, teachers
and administrators learn together as a team. Not only do they share
a common body of knowledge, they share a commitment to the
new practice and create a team spirit. Following the professional
development, they work as a team to incorporate their new learning into their instruction. The perfect schools provide abundant
evidence that school-wide professional development works. When
talking to principals from these perfect schools, we did not hear a
single administrator speak about the success of individuals pursuing their own professional development or the value of local professional development committees. In fact, several echoed the sen-
timents of one curriculum director who said, "We put an incredible amount of money into professional development but have
really worked hard to avoid the one shot deals and sending individual teachers out to workshops and classes. They don't work,
they aren't effective, and they take teachers away from kids." Although they did not deter teachers from furthering their own education and learning, they knew that what counted in the classroom
was the team professional development. In other words, they "get"
what Richard Elmore says, "Professional development is effective
only to the degree that it engages teachers and administrators in
large-scale improvement...Professional development must support
a *collective good.*"[6]

In short, collaboration breeds ownership as the school grows,
which in turn leads to greater student success.

In addition to collaboration, we have found that teachers in the
perfect school are truly different. A whole chapter is devoted to
the perfect staff. Take our word that the perfect staff is really
something special and unique. Like my son's go cart, when all the
parts work together, the whole school roars to life, student
achievement rockets ahead, and it gets the community's attention!

Conclusion

Perfect schools excel at identifying and closing gaps. This doesn't
happen by miracle or coincidence. These schools teach us an important lesson in leadership, hard work, and teamwork, a lesson

---

[6] Elmore, R., ***Bridging the Gap Between Standards and Achievement:
The Imperative for Professional Development in Education***.

learned long ago when America united the East and West in the 1860s. Writes historian Stephen Ambrose, "Next to winning the Civil War and abolishing slavery, building the first transcontinental railroad was the greatest achievement of the American people in the 19th century. It took brains, muscles and sweat in quantities and scope never before put into a single project. Most of all, it could not have been done without teamwork."[7]

Summary

This chapter has specifically focused on using data to bridge academic gaps, and has discussed related programs that good data collection and interpretation would affect. In summary, a perfect school:

- Identifies gaps in achievement among groups of students
- Builds a culture of high expectations for achievement, behavior, and success for every child
- Makes literacy the top academic priority
- Reaches out to parents and caregivers
- Extends the school day and/or year
- Updates technology and textbooks
- Assures that all teachers are highly skilled and committed to the school's mission

These strategies, if implemented, would put schools on the path to perfection.

---

[7] Ambrose, S., *Nothing Like it in the World*. New York: Simon and Schuster, 2000.

Why don't they pass a constitutional amendment prohibiting anyone from learning anything? If it works as well as the prohibition did, in five years Americans would be the smartest race of people on Earth.

Will Rogers (1879-1935)

Chapter Twelve

Financing Education

Jim Rosborg

The perfect school (1) looks at ways to redefine current financial practices to make public education maximize tax dollars for programs to help kids, (2) understands that schools are in the people business and that part of that business is the collective bargaining process, (3) looks at ways to make the funds fit the curricular programs rather than having the curricular programs fit the funds, (4) understands that school facilities are many times the rock of the community, and (5) works hard to understand local, state, and national funding to maximize revenue sources for the school.

This chapter deals with school funding, which is the single most important element in achieving the perfect school. Many say that money does not make the school, but we disagree. Class size makes a huge difference because the specific needs of many students impacts how many students a teacher can effectively instruct. The more individual attention a good teacher can give, the more success the student will have.

Outstanding facilities make an educational difference, as do student support personnel. The appearance of buildings and grounds are important too—one of the first things a good parent does before moving to a new area is drive by the school. The perception they receive about the school district is related to the quality of its buildings and grounds; that helps determine whether the parents move to that specific area.

Ironically, in our initial book (***What Every Superintendent and Principal Needs to Know***) we did not dwell on the funding issue. We talked around some funding components, such as collective bargaining and buildings and grounds, but we really didn't discuss specific funding ideas. We probably avoided the issue because funding is often difficult to talk about in a global sense since there are so many different methods of funding education throughout the United States. While we recognize and respect the uniqueness of the states' funding systems for their schools, this chapter will focus on some ideas we feel will be beneficial to the success of every school in every state. We will also suggest ideas that are costly but will improve schools. So let's look at a few funding initiatives, how these funds are managed, and what more one might do with additional funds.

Funding Initiatives

The perfect school understands that the allocation and management of revenues, with tight expense control, is the key for providing the biggest bang for the student educational buck. The school's budget is the critical core of the district's spending. The assurance that expenses do not overcome revenues is vitally important to the district's stakeholders. How is that best done? How does the perfect school use financial data to make the tough decisions about personnel, class size, professional development, and new programs implementation? How do they track effectiveness in their financial decisions? Some key knowledge components of the budget have to be understood.

- The perfect school has to understand the federal, state, and local levels where its funds are coming from to make solid budgetary predictions. Past budgets give a strong indicator of revenues that will be received this fiscal year. The same with expenses. From this starting info, budgetary adjustments are then made for the upcoming fiscal year.

- Every year, the perfect school analyzes how their resources were allocated. How has the school invested its money to impact student performance? Should certain dol-

lars be moved to other budget line items where there has
been greater academic success?

- The budget should be understandable to all key stakeholders in the district: income, expenses, and who is responsible for determining how that money is allocated.
This should be shared with the Board, parents, the media,
government officials, educators, and others involved in the
decision-making process. Many leaders in the educational
field believe that revenue allocations can be improved
when the goals are clearly articulated, so others can see
the costs and benefits associated with reaching higher
standards. Do these goals adequately reflect the special
needs of the area where the schools are located, i.e. rural,
suburban, and urban?[1]

- The perfect school understands that increased income
generally depends on increased revenues from the federal
and state level, an increase in students, and local property
growth.

- The perfect school keeps a historical record of class size at
each grade level to be able to predict where teachers are
most needed to meet student needs.

- The perfect school works closely with the district's auditor
to study current accounting practices and to determine if
changes are needed.

- The perfect school looks at whether the funds are being allocated for general education purposes or specially funded
projects.

- The perfect school understands that good people are still
the most important component to successfully financed
schools.

- The perfect school dreams of special initiatives that can
help its students raise their levels of academic success.

[1] "Insights on Educational Policy, Practice, and Research" in *Making
Educational Dollars Work: Understanding Resource Allocation*, Southwest Educational Development Laboratory, Issue # 14, November, 2001.

As this book is printed, obesity is one of the most pressing problems facing American youth. Even though this has been identified as a major problem, many school districts are faced with restricting some of their physical education programs because of the additional curricular stress to increase reading and mathematics scores. This is being done even though the Centers for Disease Control and Prevention reported in 2007 that the percentage of young Americans who are now overweight has more than tripled since 1980, and in the age group 6-19, 16 % are considered overweight.[2]

The closing of physical education classes in itself has become a funding issue because of potential revenues that school districts can now receive in the reading and math areas. Examples of this include federal and state reading grants and state-initiated summer school monies. On top of this, many children who are obese hate physical education activities because of their own lack of ability to successfully participate in group activities. This also causes discipline problems in PE classes, so school authorities prefer that students are in the academic classrooms. Here is where creative funding can help make America's youth more physically fit and, one hopes, enjoy physical development classes.

For example, America's schools might invest in a physical development program similar to Gold's Gym, Bally's, or a YMCA. These programs are based on taking a person where they are and helping them individually improve their muscle tone and cardiovascular fitness. Individual workout routines would be designed to ensure success. The activities could be set up on a rotating basis, like a workout plan three days a week one week, two days a week the next. Monitored by a physical education teacher, individual records would be shared with the student so they could continue their own improvement. On the days when these individual workout stations were not being used, other physical education activities—team sports, individual sports, and other physical development programs—could be held. The bottom line is that there needs to be a dramatic change in our emphasis on physical development activities. Obesity causes huge problems nationwide and diverts vast amounts of financial resources from education. In a 1999

---

[2] Centers for Disease Control, 1/22/07, at www.cdc.gov/nccdphp/dnpa/obesity/index.htm.

study of the costs of obesity, The Lewin Group estimated the health costs of obesity in the United States to be 102 billion dollars.[3] Think of the financial impact if just one third of these dollars were placed back into education. Thus obesity truly does impact school funding. It's just one obvious example of where schools can help students and help themselves at the same time.

How do we pay for this? It can be paid for in a variety of ways. First of all, most high schools have some type of weight training program for their athletes. Why not use the current facilities to establish a program within the regular physical education classes? Other ideas include building these plans into your budget when constructing new schools. Work with community groups to explain the need and seek donations. Hold fund raisers that include health fairs. Get your parent groups involved.

YMCA's throughout this country have been successful in getting individuals to donate money to their program's expansion. Likewise, so have schools. If schools have an outstanding plan to make students more physically fit, they can get financial support from individual business or industry in their community—or in the case of impoverished environments, through foundation and grant programs. This financial support can be further expanded by establishing a program whereby community members, including senior citizens, are given times outside the regular school day to make use of the facilities. The school becomes a partner with its community. Not only does the school help improve the physical fitness of the key stakeholders, the school also builds support for future bond issues and referenda.

I have dwelt long on the above example to show the close relationship between finance and improvement of the curriculum. Finance and curriculum go hand in hand in overall school improvement. We discussed some of these issues in other chapters in this book. Let's quickly look at a few more ways a school can expand beyond current capabilities with improved means of finance.

Universal pre-school

Early intervention is needed for students with academic difficulties. A required pre-school would greatly aid those students who do not have the financial backing to currently attend pre-school. In

---

[3] Analysis by The Lewin Group, 1999, for the Centers for Disease Control, Third National Health; and Nutrition Examination Survey.

many communities, affluent students have the opportunity to attend a pre-school setting while those who are in impoverished situations do not. This idea has been discussed in many states but unfortunately funding has not been made available. Administrators seeking the perfect school need to be proactive legislatively if their state does not provide pre-school funding. This funding initiative would be huge in bridging the academic gap, saving future educational interventions, and the solving or helping eliminate problems associated with failure in the classroom.

Extend School Day/Saturday School

This idea can help both student remediation and student enrichment. A good extended day program works with both paid individuals and volunteers. Their focus should be on individualized instruction for remediation and providing opportunities for enrichment classes. Possible programmatic offerings might be cooking, sewing, advance math and reading, basic mechanics, basic wood working, physical development, hands-on science and geography, first aid, babysitting techniques, and test preparation. Other ideas could include using the computer labs for technological training and skill development.

Resource use classes

Why not have a class that uses community resources, where students would go on field trips to places like the YMCA, other athletic facilities, government buildings, museums, libraries, nursing homes—or perhaps attend a community play production. This class would also demonstrate to students that there are many alternatives to alcohol and other drugs throughout the community and, hopefully, it would also help them develop better life skills. These activities are usually inexpensive. Many times community agencies just want to get the kids into the facilities for exposure. When there is a cost, parents generally are willing to pay a fee. The school has to take the initiative to work with the community agencies to make sure indigent kids are not left out because of their economic status.

Self-discipline programs

As our society fights some of the current problems resulting from a lack of student self-discipline, schools are going to have to make adjustments. Besides having a structured program that is student oriented, schools have to have more personnel to monitor student actions. Schools need more bus monitors, lunch room supervisors, classroom aids, resource teachers, and before- and after-school specialists. This is the only way that schools are going to be able to effectively provide the positive learning environment to help students overcome some of the current self-discipline problems we are observing. The value of additional support personnel could be extraordinary.

The question becomes how we increase funding in schools while making sure that the quality of education improves for the students in these schools. Commission after commission has pointed out the funding gap between the schools in an affluent environment and those schools in an impoverished environment.[4] The experiences we have observed also tell us that affluent communities do not want to share their tax dollars with impoverished communities. In many cases, their feeling is that they have worked hard to earn their money so they want their own children to have the maximum benefits of their local school district. What can we do? Let's look at funding from the federal, state, and local levels.

Federal Funding

The most obvious way the federal government can help is to adequately fund special education (IDEA). With the associated programmatic mandates, the funding of special education has become a black hole for school districts. Current estimates indicate that the federal government pays only 18% of the total cost of special education mandated services required of the local school districts. IDEA (Individual Disabilities Education Act) was passed initially with the intent of providing a 40% funding level. In addition, special education legislation has caused a sizeable increase in disputes that result in more hearings and litigation. If we want to positively impact funding, special education needs fewer mandates and more funding. The same holds true with the No Child Left Behind Act. School districts are finding it more difficult to balance their budgets because of the mandates of the federal government. It's time

---

[4] ***Tough Choices or Tough Times.*** National Center On Education and the Economy, Jossey-Bass, Washington, D.C., 2006, pp. 16-8.

for that same federal government to step up and adequately fund its legal mandates. The perfect school administration and staff need to be legislatively active on this issue or these black holes of funding will continue to place school districts at financial risk.

State Funding

State governments also find themselves in a difficult position. The constitution has delegated responsibility to educate kids to the states. That becomes complicated when the state legislators must also provide enough money to their schools to overcome the federal mandate deficits. State budgets are further stretched supporting their indigent population, health needs, transportation issues, prisons, natural resources, security, and payroll. Any growth in educational funding is going to have to involve a tax increase or tax shift, both nightmares for legislators. The tax increase can mean the loss of the next election, which begs the question, which is really the priority, education or re-election?

Tax increases can come from many different sources. Do you increase the corporate income tax? Do you add taxes to businesses? Both of these taxes negatively impact the business/industrial climate. Do you increase the personal income tax? This can limit the purchasing power of the consumer and also negatively impact business/industry. The increase in income and sales taxes also has a huge impact on individuals on a fixed income. Even if the legislators want to increase school funding, the decision is tough because they know they will receive the wrath of the voter. Still, these tough decisions are going to have to be made. In many cases, there must be more money provided to schools for services and facilities.

Local Funding

Local educational leaders face a similar dilemma. Do they attempt to increase the local property tax? Do they cut services to students when the budget cannot be balanced? Do they lay off good teachers and cut needed programs? (The last thing school leaders want to do is cut programs.)

During the last eight years that I served as superintendent, even though we dealt with decreasing revenues, we didn't eliminate a single program. We felt that once a program was closed down, it was very seldom renewed. A good school district protects its programs for the consistency of the curriculum. As we discussed in another chapter, the perfect school does not continually change its reading and math programs without a research base. The perfect school makes sure that the funds fit the programs, not that the programs fit the funds.

What else can the local school district do? We feel the district must work hard to protect monies for students and facilities while being fair to the staff when it comes to salaries. This becomes particularly touchy when the district gets an influx of new money, as happens with the roller coaster ride of up and down funding that occurs in education. More state revenues, more funds—and vice versa. To initially distribute all new revenue for salaries is a public relations nightmare and terrible for long-term financial planning. Education is a people business so some of this money is going to have to go to salaries. As a matter of fact, the perfect school wants staff members to have good salaries and benefits while keeping the schools financially solvent. The amount for salaries becomes part of the local district's responsibility through collective bargaining. The main goal is to reach contract agreements with the staff so that successful learning can take place. The key is for all parties to remain professional and be respectful of each other's needs and to never try to embarrass each other in the negotiation process. The perfect school leadership team remains professional even when the employees waiver from this goal. They lead by example and negotiate ethically while remaining positive. The perfect school sets the ground work for successful negotiation techniques, including:

- The understanding that all individuals in the workforce want to get an increase in salaries. To be able to maintain increases in the salaries leads to increased satisfaction with the work environment which can lead to higher test scores.

- The understanding that neither the employment groups nor the Board are professional negotiators so mistakes in the process can be made.

- Open communication that includes factual data on the finances is a key component to a successful resolution.

- The understanding that there will be some emotionalism and adversity in negotiations, but working through to a successful settlement allows better relations to develop for the duration of the contract.

- Members of the perfect school's negotiation teams will shake hands and smile once the settlement is reached.

The collective bargaining process is extremely important, but only one of the many avenues of the local district's financial responsibility. There are many other actions that pay off. For example, scheduling workshops outside the regular school day keeps the teacher in the classroom, resulting in a more consistent learning environment and improved testing results. Teachers are happy to get the extra pay for the workshops. The district saves dollars in substitute teacher pay while helping students.

Other avenues that can financially help local districts include:

- Establishing local educational foundations to use monies for enriching programs and helping students in need.

- Working with service groups and parents to donate school supplies and clothing. (In Belleville, Illinois, we had service groups that donated items like shoes, eye glasses, coats, and hearing aids.)

- Working with business/industry to secure donations. (Another example from Belleville was the Boeing Corporation's donation of 600 used computers to the district. This single act saved the district thousands of dollars at a time when the district was having financial challenges because of the decreased revenues. The computers were much appreciated and well used by the students.)

- Extending tort immunity laws to our schools, even if they were limited to making the loser pay court costs and lawyer fees. All schools are plagued by frivolous lawsuits. The amount of time and energy spent by the district's attorneys, the administrators, and other staff members is exorbitant. Making the adjudicated loser in the case pay for legal fees and court costs incurred by the districts would limit the number of trivial suits, saving the taxpayers millions of dollars. Even better would be tort legislation that would limit the amount of the awards. The perfect school administrator should be working pro-actively on this issue.

Invest in your buildings and grounds

Too often, when school districts are having financial difficulties, they let the normal repair of their buildings and grounds slide, sometimes to a dismal state. What lack of foresight. Usually the number of students enrolled helps determine your funding level. If a building is in ill repair, then parents, given a choice, won't move into the area. People also judge the quality of instruction by the appearance of the buildings. What are some long-range goals you can set for your buildings and grounds?

- Keep your buildings clean and your grounds in neat order. This is a low-cost item that is huge in the perception that key stakeholders have of the school. Get your students involved in the effort so they have pride in their school. (A word of caution here. Never leave students unattended when involved with these activities and never involve chemicals or other caustic substances when students are volunteering to help.)

- In much of the United States there is a need to air condition the buildings. If you have a long-range plan, you can make this happen. Your learning environment will improve immensely.

- Make your buildings energy efficient. Replace old windows. Lower high ceilings. Put in new energy-efficient lighting and heating systems. Brighten up your hallways and classrooms. Replace bathroom fixtures. Renovate the school office. All of these things can happen through planning and effort.

- Add new playground equipment. In many cities school grounds are part of the local park system. Enhance your school and your city with new playground equipment. This is a popular project for many parent groups since they realize that their children will directly benefit from their efforts.

- Get a new flagpole. What brings a better focus on the school than the flag? Schools are symbols of our democracy.

- In the classrooms, get current computer hardware. Replace slate boards with white boards. Upgrade the shades. Paint the rooms.

- Make cafeterias and gymnasiums attractive. Add curtains and other sound control materials to both. Paint them in school colors. These are two areas where the stakeholders in the community spend a great deal of time. Make them more attractive.

All of this costs money, of course, but the overall value to the school is well worth the expense. Bond issues, cooperative funding programs, grant revenues, and donations are all options for revenue. A general community brainstorming session on revenue sources often opens up unique opportunities.

The more revenues that can be generated for your district, the more opportunities students have. Districts lose thousands of dollars in revenues by not seeking grants from government agencies, foundations, and business/industry. While a district has to be careful not to allow the grant to control their curriculum, they must provide ways of enhancing the program.

For example, as superintendent I was part of a team that helped our district secure a $2,000,000 National Science Foundation Grant for teaching math problem-solving techniques. This was very instrumental in helping improve math scores across the board. The opportunities are there. Use them to enhance your curriculum and school district. Join with other districts and hire a grant writer. This should more than pay for that individual's salary and could lead to huge dividends for your program. Grants are generally competitive. Submit them professionally and do not let failures get in your way of forging ahead to take advantage of future opportunities.

Financially reward good schools

Education many times seems to consider funding just the reverse of business. In business, if one works hard and has good leadership, an excellent staff, and a good product, the business generally will make more money. Not in education. If the staff works hard, has skilled teachers and excellent administrators, and the students score high on tests, a school receives less national and state funds than if its students do terribly on the tests. By scoring high, the school isn't eligible for federal Comprehensive Reform grant money under Title I or most of the support money under the No Child Left Behind Act. School districts are punished for doing a good job. This philosophy has to change.

School districts doing a good job should serve as professional development models and should be financially rewarded for their efforts. This incentive should be taken to the teaching level. If a teacher shows consistently higher test score results compared to corresponding teachers who have the same level of demographics, this teacher should be financially rewarded. Let's put money behind success and see what happens.

Schools need to understand the importance of good fiscal management. The perfect school understands the importance of controlling everyday expenses. It understands that schools are big businesses that deal with budgets that are for the most part derived from taxpayers' money. The perfect school becomes expert in fiscal affairs. It understands its accounts, bonding, shopping for loans, comparing prices of goods and services, school law and the impact of litigation, preventive maintenance, energy conservation, revenue resources, and inventory control.

The perfect school understands that the effort made to enhance revenues and control expenses is critical to its success. The perfect school administrator understands that one must be legislative proactive to achieve these goals. The special education funding issue alone (18-40%) would solve most financial deficits and/or provide the funds for most needed improvements discussed in this chapter. While some expenses are not able to be controlled (like special education), most are. Spending dollars in the right areas for the right reason sometimes results in long-term savings. For example, better health and social support along with an effective pre-school program can bring less truancies, fewer students needing special education services, and less involvement with the police.

Planning, community brainstorming, business partnership, active parent groups, and foundations can be utilized to find revenues and change the overall school climate. A balanced budget requires planning and tough decisions. It can be achieved while still protecting the good programs the district has implemented. The perfect school understands these concepts and moves forward.

Chapter Thirteen

Total Curriculum

Jim Rosborg

The perfect school (1) uses its curriculum as a tool to continually look at the academic program's strengths and weaknesses, (2) gets input from its staff and key stakeholders on all major curricular decisions, (3) aligns its curriculum to state standards, (4) adds inter-disciplinary teaching techniques into its instruction, (5) provides alternatives to retention, (6) incorporates hands-on teaching techniques, and (7) focuses its instruction on the needs of the individual student.

The perfect school understands that its curriculum is the guiding force for instruction both today and in the future. How the curriculum is designed and implemented is the center of how successful a school district is and to what degree student learning is successfully impacted. This chapter will look at curriculum and debate whether or not we are headed in the right direction. We will explore what kids need to know in today's society to be successful citizens. We will defend American education while taking a hard look at possible ways we can improve the process.

In this chapter we are going to recognize some of the current strengths in school curriculum, explore some of the current weaknesses, and identify changes needed to improve the total curriculum for general student improvement, beyond just test scores. Improving test scores is of course important, but as important is how we teach our students, what we teach them, and whether we instill a good work study ethic in them—then the test scores will naturally rise. So the curriculum must include teaching students how to find information, not just recall or reiterate it. All of that is complicated by the fact that kids come from diverse cultural and academic backgrounds

Many excellent efforts are taking place in schools to improve curriculum. Below are some of the good things happening nationwide that should be celebrated and used as foundations of future academic success.

Current Strengths

During most of the past century teachers remained relatively isolated within their own classroom. In many schools, teachers even had different textbooks from other teachers across the hall, or at the same grade level, or teaching in the same subject area. With the more recent movement towards standards-based education, teachers are spending more time collaborating in the development of their lessons, their modes of assessment, and how they are going to communicate with key stakeholders. They are teaming more to share effective ways of improving instructions.

Curriculum problems haven't, of course, disappeared. In fact, they may be more common than we would like to believe. I recently received an email from a colleague in which he discussed strategies to bring his district in line in several areas. He wrote:

> During your presentation you talked briefly about report cards and changing to a common way of reporting. As luck would have it, Wednesday afternoon I was given the task of heading the committee that will tackle this very item. We have multiple (K-5) elementary and (6-8) middle schools. No two schools have the same report card. In fact, several buildings have different report cards at the same grade level. It is very confusing for staff and parents. We also have several different calendars. A building or grade level could issue grades on quarters, semesters, or trimesters, plus (we have) problems at the middle school where multiple teachers are giving grades for the same subject. Teaming is great, but if three teachers are giving a math grade, who does the parent talk to when their child isn't doing well? Besides that, each teacher has

different grading scales and each school has a different honor roll with different subjects being taught. My charge is to develop a plan and timeline to address these problems.

This scenario represents a situation that is still too common in school districts. The good thing is that educators are realizing that this scenario itself is a problem. School after school is integrating its curriculum horizontally across subject matter and vertically between grade levels. They are differentiating their instruction to meet the needs of students of diverse abilities. They are looking at ways to revise their curriculum, the ways that it is taught, and how it is assessed. Educators throughout this country are tackling curricular issues of inconsistency, using positive articulation methods to bring consistency to the assessment system. A perfect school setting allows teacher autonomy to improve their classroom while developing a uniform assessment system that articulates the areas needed for instructional improvement.

In today's society, it is readily apparent that teachers, administrators, school boards, parents, and the community all want to have a voice in choosing the school curriculum. Many times people associated with these groups have their own agenda in the decision-making process. While there have been huge improvements in the way schools are attempting to involve these key stakeholders, problems still exist. The question becomes what to do and how to do it. Procedurally, we suggest the following:

- Collaborate with your teachers at their respective professional levels. If there is a question about gifted education, talk to the gifted teacher. If there is a need for improvement in the area of math, involve the teachers of math. Make them feel part of the decision-making process.

- Set up a committee. In doing so, be up front that the final results of the committee should be consistent with district curricular goals and can not negatively impact other areas of the curriculum. Let the committee know its mission. While administration needs to lead, there also must be respected teacher leaders on the committee. Also decide if individuals outside of the professional staff should be included. How much involvement should union leaders have? That depends upon whether the successful changes involve the union. That's a professional judgment at the district level. (While I served as Superintendent in Belleville, Illinois, we had 22 functioning committees that ranged from boundary changes to curriculum to PTAs to science fairs.) The process works. It takes a great deal of planning on the administrator's part, but it gives key stakeholders the feeling of being part of the change process.

- Lay out all the current scenarios for the committee, then pursue one issue at a time. How are you going to get ownership from the rest of the staff on the issues discussed in committee? Input has to be allowed from staff members outside the committee to obtain this ownership. That ownership generally determines whether the committee's results are part of the future curricular design.

- Let the committee know that your efforts are in building consensus in the decision-making process, with the full knowledge that the final decision might possibly be different than the current practices they are using. What's more, we recommend the collaborative method where you work for consensus building in each issue as opposed to having your committee vote on each issue. What does that mean? The leader must recognize the direction the committee is going, determine what the consensus is, and not let a vocal minority opinion dictate. The person who is leading the committee must have the ability to determine what that consensus is. If the leader of the committee realizes the committee is headed in a direction different from district goals, intervention (with an explanation) is immediately required.

- In this committee process, it is imperative in a collaborative effort that administrators give teachers time to meet and discuss educational issues both with other teachers at their grade level and with teachers at other grade levels. This has been a strength of the No Child Left Behind Act. By having required testing in reading and in math in grades 3-8, this has forced school districts to open up dialogue between teachers at these grade levels, so that test scores improve. Going into these meetings, administrators should have issues identified for discussion, but there should also be time for brainstorming and discussing ways to improve instruction. These meetings should be used not only for problem identification in the curriculum but also for problem solving so that there is an improvement in the learning process and in the student results.

- Teacher Advisory Committees are becoming more and more important in the collaborative movement and in the curricular change process. No longer can top down leadership by itself be effective in a school setting. It's imperative that staff members have a sense of ownership in both policy and curriculum development. Likewise, in dealing with a teacher's union/teacher association, rather than waiting until union/teacher association officials come to administrators with issues about the school or district, regularly scheduled meetings should be set up in which the administration and staff can discuss issues. This is the only way that a collaborative environment can take place. Frequent and regular meetings tend to reduce emotions. The framework of these meetings should be established so that individuals are free to bring up and identify any perceived problem with the understanding that once the problem is identified, the committee will be working together to find solutions. People are more likely to be problem identifiers than good problem solvers. By establishing an environment of problem solving within the committee, this may well impact the results that come out of the committee action. As the leader of the committee, it's counterproductive to accept a statement like "You make the decision. That's what you get the big bucks for." If people want to be involved in the decision-making process, they have to be involved in the solutions, not just problem identification. When this procedure is followed, attitudes and district morale improve. This helps replace the traditional negative teacher lounge talks with discussions about what is best for kids. This is a goal of the perfect school.

Curricular Alignment of State Standards

With the passage of the No Child Left Behind Act in 2002, one of the positive results of the legislation was that schools, districts, and even state boards have had to focus more on standards and curricular alignment. It is essential that schools establish consistent local assessments that coordinate with state and national assessments. All three forms of assessment need to be aligned with similar standards. In the alignment process, benchmarks need to be established for these identified standards. Benchmarks are the points that are established to determine if a student meets the requirements of a standard. There is still a great deal of work needed to be done in the standards movement nationwide. For example, Illinois initially identified so many standards that it was impossible to teach each established objective. Efforts have been made to rectify this situation by narrowing the focus of instruction to an achievable framework. States throughout this country need to focus their standards in such a way that instructional goals are achievable. A framework needs to be developed so teachers can focus on the standards that are going to be assessed. When this happens, it will be possible to establish benchmarks and assessment instruments in such a way that effective instructions can take place.

Another positive impact of the No Child Left Behind Act has been the increased emphasis on reading, writing, and arithmetic. Districts nationwide have added instructional time in these core academic areas. We have known for years that if an elementary student is having problems with the basics of reading and math, they are more likely to have problems in other academic areas, such as social studies and science. This emphasis on reading and math helps all academic areas.

The increased use of technology in the schools has definitely improved student learning over the last decade. In the past, students who were expected to be future leaders in business and industry were getting virtually no technological preparation in their formative educational years. The school computers that were used were often so out of date that current instructionally required software could not be used. This is changing. Today the instructional emphasis is starting to focus more on networking than software. Schools are striving to keep their hardware up to date and students are now having the opportunity to develop their technological skills in the K-12 setting. Computer labs and individual student computers, with modern hardware, continue to be added throughout the United States. We are also seeing wireless networking in the schools, mobile labs, and one-to-one laptop initiatives. In addition to the individual computers in the classrooms, new opportunities have been created for schools, like creative writing labs, technology nights for parents, and staff development activities. Technology is being used to improve reading and math skills and enhance geography, history, and science while enriching the total learning environment throughout a student's school career.

We are now seeing curricular plans being mapped out in a way that focuses on coordinating instruction. These curricular maps provide a framework for learning and also allow teachers to focus on realizable standards. They often include uniform assessments and follow-up instructional activities for student improvement.

Finally, there seems to be more communication going on between high schools, colleges, and universities. More and more high schools are able to offer advanced students dual credit courses and advanced placement courses. This allows students who are the future in academic leadership to move forward at a more rapid pace. It also offers preparatory coursework so they are better trained for the workforce.

Current Weaknesses

While the focus on reading and math has helped improve core academic areas, it is hurting other academic areas. The perfect school will need to reach a midpoint in curricular development. Despite the negative reaction to education in many parts of our own society, American education is admired throughout the world. Students flock to the United States to get a good education. For us to continue to be educational leaders, we must continue to recognize student strengths, whether we are talking about academics, sports, intelligence, creativity, or other skills related to the specific individual. To do that the total curriculum must still include components such as science, social studies, daily physical education, fine/practical arts, music, vocational education, and gifted education, along with reading and math. There must continue to be a rigorous core curriculum in high schools nationwide. For those students interested in the career/technical fields, a good vocational program is also essential.

Vocational education should include a variety of opportunities such as auto shop, wood shop, metal shop, electrical shop, plumbing, and industrial technology. Common sense tells us that these classes make school more enjoyable, pique student creativity, help further recognize student strengths, and improve student achievement; that reading and/or math should be used in all of the above subjects, and that we can alleviate this concern by implementing inter-disciplinary instructional techniques in all classrooms.

It is the same interdisciplinary teaching that is a weakness in the curriculum now. For example, math and reading concepts should be integrated into science and social studies lessons. Such as a geography lesson that incorporates math skills in determining how far it is between point A, point B, and point C or the longitudinal differences between an identified location in the United States and an identified location in Asia. Reading strategies can be incorporated into required reading in science and social studies. A good professional development program focusing on curriculum integration can result in the improvement of instruction.

Provide alternatives for retention

In a discussion with Dennis O'Neill, a school psychologist in Illinois, we talked about a very common occurrence with kids, especially in poverty environments, regarding academic achievement. Sammy is an example. A seven-year-old second grader, he has never repeated a grade. He is from a poverty-level home where both parents are present, as well as an aunt and two older cousins. Sammy has been referred by his teacher for a case study evaluation for possible special education services because of behavioral concerns as well as academic deficits. He sits near the teacher because he is disruptive, does not adhere to classroom rules, refuses to complete his work, and hollers in class. His academic concerns include reading and written language skills at a first grade level. He has difficulty remembering sight words. He needs to have directions read orally to him. His sentence structure is poor and he has little understanding of punctuation and capitalization.

Sammy's is a very common description in the referrals of some students in the second grade. The students come to school in kindergarten with splintered or even impoverished vocabulary and comprehension skills, and have little or no pre-academic training. They do not have a good comprehension of spoken language and consequently miss concepts and basic skills in kindergarten and first grade. Nonetheless, they learn their letters and some sight words and with good attention from their teachers, they maintain with marginal skills through first grade. In second grade, however, their deficits become exaggerated because more reading comprehension is required. They still lag behind in phonetic and sight word skills, and they continue to have comprehension problems because they just cannot catch up to the increasingly difficult material. Although Sammy has never been retained, many of his peers have. And it is likely that Sammy will be retained at the end of second grade. We've also seen his frustration in the classroom spawn into a variety of behavioral concerns, most of which can be answered by the typical student question, "What am I going to do all day? I can't do the work and I have to stay in the classroom!"

What curriculum adjustments could be made in the district to accommodate and help these students? The perfect school makes every effort not to retain students. Instead, it would research the impact on students if it developed a first to second grade transition class that specifically targeted students with environmentally-influenced deficits in reading and written language, as well as inadequate vocabulary and comprehension skills. The program could be an extension of first grade, with an emphasis on language enrichment, plus reading, writing, and arithmetic. The class should also focus on developing work-study habits and other behavioral interventions. A class like this would prevent the student from experiencing the stigma of retention. We know that early intervention helps overcome reading and math deficits. Every class the student takes would deal with reading and math.

We need to provide the support necessary early on to give the student the opportunity to succeed. The older the student gets, the broader the learning deficiencies and the more difficult it is to remediate. Sad to say, if we do not intervene at an early age, many students' main goals would be to simply survive in school until they are old enough to drop out. These same students become disciplinary problems and truants until that magic drop-out age occurs. The percent of prisoners in our penal system that are high school dropouts is astounding. In fact, The National Dropout Prevention Center/Network located at Clemson University estimates that 82% of the prisoners in the United States are high school dropouts.[1] The Network goes on to say that high school dropouts are four times more likely to be unemployed, make less money, and are more likely to receive some form of public assistance. To help alleviate this problem, we need to focus on early academic intervention along with alternative educational studies to at least give these students a chance to succeed.

Incorporate Hands–On and Project-based Learning

The perfect school should implement into the curriculum time for teachers to do more hands-on and project-based learning. An example of this would be to have actual maps on the desk during a geography lesson so the student can directly work with the material. In science, the student would have supplies at their table to conduct an experiment. In math, the use of manipulatives would give the student hands-on learning experiences. Many teachers would like to implement more of these types of learning; however, the time frame that educators have to cover the required curriculum does not allow them to do as much as they want. By allowing students to have more hands-on or project-based learning, students are being given the opportunity to incorporate multiple levels of learning. Also, by giving students this opportunity, they will be acquiring the skills and abilities they need when they enter the workforce. In addition, kids today are more adept at hands-on learning because of the environment in which they live. Schools are competing against Sony's Play Station 3, I-pods, camera cell phones, and a multitude of other video games. Our schools must incorporate into their instruction things like smart boards, Power Point, hands-on science, math, and geography. The project-based learning concept not only brings hands-on into the lesson, but also higher order thinking skills.

---

[1] National Dropout Prevention Center/Network, Clemson University, 2006, www.dropoutprevention.org.

Earlier in this chapter we discussed vocational education courses as opportunities to improve student interest. Many countries throughout the world have implemented a vocational learning track for those students who have more interest in skill areas than the core academic subjects. The need for these skill positions in the United States is dramatic. Sad to say, many school districts are lessening their emphasis on vocational education to meet the mandates created under the No Child Left Behind Act. Our curricular focus needs to establish a balance between core academic areas and core vocational areas. If we are going to compete globally with countries like India and China, we are going to have to maintain both a strong core curriculum and a strong vocational curriculum that directly coincides with a top-of-the-line industrial training system. After all, in reality some of our very best skilled technicians may not have traditional academic strengths in the core subject areas.

We feel that instruction should be focused on the student and not on the subject. Many teachers today, especially at the middle school and high school level, become so focused on the material they are presenting that they lose focus of the needs of their students. In the perfect school, we need to focus instruction on the student by examining where the student's academic achievement level is, then move them forward. No longer is a general lecture a successful mode of instruction. No longer can we expect every student in the classroom to be on the same material at the same time. No longer can we expect students to be engaged in classroom activities if we are doing repetitive lessons and repetitive classroom activities every week. Students have to know that the instructor cares about their learning process and is genuinely concerned about student success. We have to take responsibility in the classroom to keep the student focused and engaged in the learning process.

While we have made many positive strides in the communication between colleges, universities, and school districts, there is a great deal more that needs to be accomplished to improve curriculum. The perfect school will improve planning between all entities regarding student-teacher activities, mentoring of new teachers, mentoring new administrators, and professional development.

The Gifted Student

Major studies and academic planning also need to take place to refocus instructional activities of the gifted student. In times of budget crisis, many states are lessening or even ending funding for academically-talented students. This is simply wrong. These kids are going to be our future leaders in many areas of our society. At the perfect school, learning challenges should be continually developed for gifted students in every grade level, K-12. These students need to again be a major focus of instruction. We should not be satisfied that these kids simply meet state academic standards. The perfect school establishes programs for these kids and helps them move toward academic and career excellence.

Discipline

In these times another major concern affecting curriculum is the lack of discipline in many schools throughout the nation. What is causing this? Many educators would say that schools have been harnessed in their ability to discipline by laws passed by legislators and by case law from the courts. These same educators would say that the lack of self-discipline being taught in the home is also a major problem.

These reasons are all part of the problem, but the perfect school has to take responsibility for disciplining students while they are at school. For example, every teacher should monitor students between each class period. Every staff member should assume total school responsibility when it comes to discipline. No longer can a teacher just deal with discipline issues in their own classroom. It takes the teamwork of *all* staff members to control student discipline. Administration has to back the staff and provide consistent consequences for inappropriate behavior. The bottom line is that when a school loses its disciplinary control of students, it also loses its ability to improve its curriculum and its assessment results. A good disciplinary structure is a key component to the implementation of a successful curricular program.

While it is impossible to discuss all aspects of curriculum in one chapter of this book, our goal has been to establish that in the perfect school curriculum the focus of student improvement must become a predominant and major focus of the planning process. The perfect school considers curriculum development and revisions a major artery of student academic success. The perfect school uses every available resource to improve the instructional environment. The perfect school sets curricular goals and corresponding timelines, then it sets out to achieve those goals. Once the goals are achieved, other goals are set so that there is a continual emphasis on improvement. The perfect school takes successful curricular trends and uses them, but also identifies weaknesses in the curriculum and makes needed changes by using a collaborative mode of leadership.

Instead of trying to come up and pontificate on what literature is, you need to talk with children, to teachers, and make sure they get poetry in the curriculum early.

Rita Dove (1952-   )

BIOGRAPHIES

For more biographical information, photos, and speaking programs, please check http://www.superintendents-and-principals.com.

Jim Rosborg

Dr. Jim Rosborg currently serves as Program Coordinator for External Graduate Programs at McKendree College, Lebanon, Illinois. He also is instructor of graduate courses in education. In addition, Rosborg is a frequent speaker on topics such as data management, NCLB, school law, and "Bridging the Academic Gap." This is his 35th year in education, having retired from Belleville, Illinois District #118 after serving as a teacher, coach, guidance counselor, principal, assistant superintendent, and superintendent prior to his current position. He received his doctorate from Southern Illinois University at Edwardsville in 1994.

Dr. Rosborg has received numerous awards including the "Illinois Master Teacher" award, the Illinois State Board of Education "Those Who Excel" award, the Illinois State Board of Education "Break the Mold" award, the Boy Scouts of America Russell C. Hill award for outstanding contribution to character development, and the 2004 Illinois Superintendent of the Year award. Besides his recent collaboration with Max McGee and Jim Burgett in writing the books *What Every Superintendent and Principal Needs to Know* and *The Perfect School*, Rosborg has published articles about dealing with children with AIDs in the classroom and adjustments needed to successfully implement the 2002 No Child Left Behind Act.

Jim Rosborg is a proud husband, father, and grandparent having been married to Nancy for 31 years. Together, they have three children: Mike (married to Wendy, with grandson Bradley), Kyle (married to Barbi), and Carol.

Max McGee

Glenn W. "Max" McGee has held positions in public schools from substitute teacher in Lebanon, New Hampshire, to State Superintendent of Education in Springfield, Illinois. He has taught middle school; coached high school; served as an elementary principal, and been superintendent of three high-achieving school districts. In addition, he is a past President of the Illinois Teachers Retirement System. He is currently Superintendent of Schools in Wilmette District 39 in Wilmette, Illinois, and a Senior Research Fellow at the Northern Illinois University Center for Governmental Studies. Max is presently an active member of the Board of Directors of the Great Books Foundation, the Golden Apple Board Foundation, and the United Cerebral Palsy of Greater Chicago.

A graduate of Dartmouth College and holder of a Ph. D. from the University of Chicago, Max has devoted his studies and career to improving teaching and learning for all students. Max has presented at the national conferences of the American Education Research Association, Association for Supervision and Curriculum Development, and National Association for the Education of Young Children, in addition to other national and statewide conferences and events. He has written articles and papers about computer technology, assessment, and educational leadership. He is currently working on publishing a scholarly, comprehensive study of high-performing, high-achieving schools in Illinois called *Closing the Achievement Gap: Lessons from the Golden Spike Schools* and completing development of a product and process that enables school leaders to benchmark their performance with similar districts.

Max's wife, Jan Fitzsimmons, runs the College Readiness Program for the Associated Colleges of Illinois and directs the Junior/Seniors Scholars youth. Their oldest boy, Mike, is employed as a technician, and the youngest, Joey, attends Barrington Middle School. They also care for Jessica, a very special young woman who is a junior at Northern Illinois. In addition to running one of the top school districts in Illinois, Max runs in marathons and is a competitive triathlete, finishing second in his age group in the 2002 Lake Geneva Extreme Triathlon.

Jim Burgett

Jim Burgett is a veteran educator and public speaker. Jim was named the "Illinois Superintendent of the Year" by the American Association of School Administrators and "Administrator of the Year" by the Illinois Association for Educational Office Professionals. He has received numerous honors and recognition for his leadership and skills as a motivator. Jim serves on many boards for the State of Illinois, various professional organizations, the Editorial Board for an educational publisher, and several community organizations.

He is the recipient of the Award of Excellence from the Illinois State Board of Education, was named a Paul Harris Fellow by Rotary International, and is currently President of his local Chamber of Commerce.

After earning a B.S. degree in education, with a minor in chemistry, at the University of Wisconsin-Platteville, Jim earned his M.S. and C.A.S. degrees at Northern Illinois University. Jim has continued his educational training and currently writes and presents administrative academies for several states.

Education has been the cornerstone of his career. Jim has been a teacher of grades five through twelve and a principal of elementary, middle school, and high school. He has served as the Superintendent of the Elizabeth Community Unit School District, the River Ridge Community Unit School District, and the Highland Community Unit School District, all in Illinois. He is frequently published by many professional journals, speaks across the country to a variety of organizations, and has keynoted at most major educational conferences in Illinois.

Jim Burgett is known for his practical leadership. He consults many districts, leads strategic planning sessions, and has been a leader in such areas as school construction, administrative standards, and effective teaching strategies.

Jim Burgett's wife, Barbara, is a medical records specialist for a senior citizen service complex in Highland. Jim and Barb have three children and five grandchildren.

INDEX

The Buck Stops With Us!

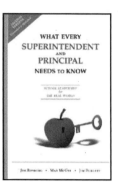

Jim Rosborg, Max McGee, and Jim Burgett

Contents: School Leadership; Civic Leadership and Ethics; Business Basics for School Leaders; Communications; Building and Sustaining Trust; Planning; Expert Knowledge; Building Internal Capacity; Visionary Leadership; Successful Teaching and Learning; Adventures in Innovation; Taking Care of You; Standards, Assessment, and Accountability, and Case Studies in Real World Leadership. **ISBN 0910167214 / Trade Paperback / $24.95.**

Second edition, released in January, 2007

> For more details, see
> **www.superintendents-and-principals.com**

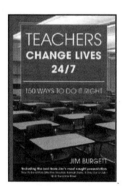

TEACHERS CHANGE LIVES 24/7

Jim Burgett

Read the testimonials, a sample chapter, and Jim's credentials at the website above and you'll see why the stories, passion, and fun that he has shared on the lecture circuit for a decade has principals and superintendents buying the book by the box load to help inject purpose, pride, and zest into their schools and districts. **ISBN 0910167915 / Trade Paperback / $15**

Scheduled publication date: March, 2007

> Education Communication Unlimited,
> P.O. Box 845, Novato, CA 94948
> or order@superintendents-and-principals.com